Unforgettable Memories

Unforgettable Memories

Swami Purnamritananda Puri

Mata Amritanandamayi Center, San Ramon
California, United States

Unforgettable Memories
By Swami Purnamritananda Puri

Published by:
Mata Amritanandamayi Center
P.O. Box 613
San Ramon, CA 94583-0613 USA
Tel: (510) 537-9417

In India:
www.amritapuri.org
inform@amritapuri.org

In Europe:
www.amma-europe.org

In US:
www.amma.org

Dedication

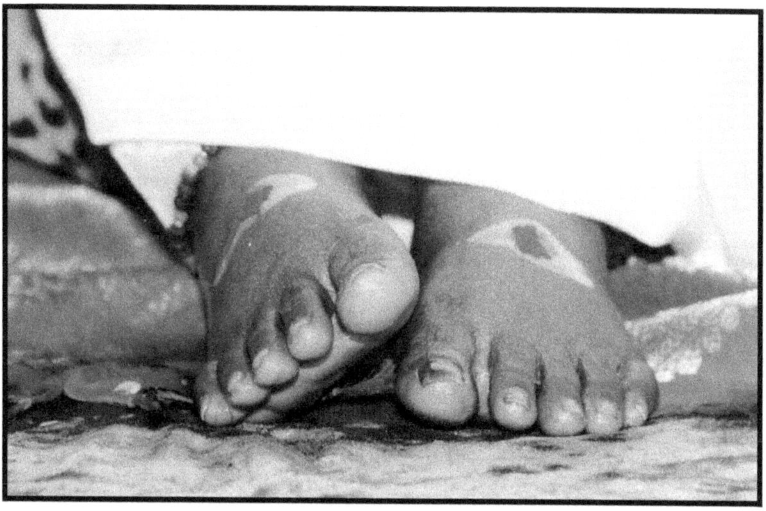

I humbly offer this book at the sacred feet of my Satguru,
Śrī Mātā Amṛtānandamayi Devī.

Contents

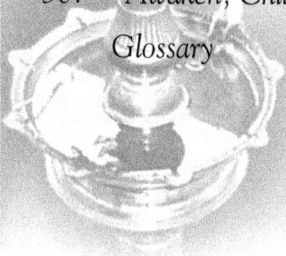

Preface

GREAT GURUS ROUSE the colossal trees slumbering in the tiny seeds. Amma transforms sharp, hard stones into sparkling diamonds. Deep in every heart lies a babe that, thrashing its hands and legs, cries "Mother! Mother!" Through her touch, Amma awakens that child-like innocence.

There may well be a thousand meanings in a *mahātma's* [great soul's] every utterance. The silence, glance and smile amid her words are all enfolded by a thousand petals. As each of these petals unfurls, a profusion of memories awakens... unforgettable and revitalizing remembrances that outlast death.

We live in an age that is proving intolerable even to the all-enduring Mother Earth. Its horrors visit us as the swell of a tsunami and the vortex of a tornado. The intellectual balks, seeing the nightmare on the brink of a catastrophe. Amma comes as the cool kiss on the forehead, the consoling caress, the deluge of love in a fevered heart.

Standing behind the telescope, man sees the black holes a thousand light years away, but he fails to see those within himself. Amma illumines these dark caverns.

The barriers of time and place are no problems for Amma. As the Mother of the Universe, she knows that the pain of the soul is the same, anytime, anywhere. In her presence, hearts broken by past experiences and conditioning enjoy peace. They become as expansive as the universe. The cosmic individual thus comes into being.

Memories of being led by Amma from the dense jungle of the intellect to the shady bower of the heart have been woven into stories that speak of an alchemy, which can transmute even dross into gold. This book contains memorable parables of how Amma, the Satguru, transmits to the disciple secrets that no philosophy can explicate.

A short note on language – In keeping with common convention, this book uses the masculine pronoun when referring to God in order to avoid such clumsy constructions as "He / She / It;" it goes without saying that the Supreme transcends all gender labels. The feminine pronoun has been used to refer to the Guru in honor of the female body Amma has assumed. The Indian words used in the book are explained in the Glossary.

In Amma's Lap

1

O GODDESS OF the Universe, may I start writing? How will I write? How can this quill pen write of its own accord? How can I write on matters about which the tongue cannot even speak?

I never thought You would present matters so clearly, things I had never imagined even once, secrets of life beyond the power of imagination! I cannot understand in what way I am deserving of this! It must be Your almighty grace – to what else can I attribute all these?

Jupiter has made two full revolutions since You erased all my preconceptions and entered my heart. It all seems so unbelievable, like a dream. I have not been able to fully understand Your glory. If the soaring satellite, orbiting in the vast skies, is unable to understand even one planet fully, how can the ego fathom the endless sights surrounding it? They will deflate the ego! This human satellite that was being drawn to the star that is Amma was ignorant of its awesome magnitude.

How long it took me to reach the expansive view that she whom I regarded as my mother, the mother who would remain mine alone, was the Mother of all! Today I know that her lap is as wide as the cosmos. A scientist who has started studying a planet gets confounded when he sees a thousand stars through a telescope.

Amma is not a phenomenon that one can fathom within a lifetime. She is a treasure-trove of endless secrets that cannot be discovered, no matter how many lifetimes one spends studying her. She is a purity the mind can never know, the intellect can never discern.

There are many intellectuals in today's world who pretend not to see what they can see with naked eyes. They should be pitied, for they cannot see what ought to be seen. We must wipe away the dirt from the mirror of our minds, which is supposed to reflect the world as it is. The distorted reflection may not necessarily be caused by the object being reflected; it may be caused by flaws in the mirror. It is because of the distorted mind-mirror that we lose the vision of Oneness.

It was with such a mind-mirror that I first reached Amma many years ago. She smelted the splintered fragments of my mind in the furnace of love, purified it and recast it through teachings on Oneness. You who give the rough boulders of human minds the polish and smoothness of whitened stones, using only the consoling caresses of compassion's unceasing flow, without subjecting them to the blazing flames of anger—how can one say that you are not God? What good deeds did I do in my previous lives to deserve these showers of blessings?

I never imagined life could be so beautiful. I never thought God's love would overflow all boundaries. Before meeting Amma, I had certain notions about life. Often, there is a yawning gap between those ideas and reality. How can I deny it? Amma's challenge to accept everything as the Lord's *prasād* has lent me strength and awakened my self-confidence.

Amma reminded me that there are thousands in the world who are suffering. The experiences of those early days with Amma must have been a training to develop a heart that understands the pains of others, and a mind that melts upon hearing the sorrows of others.

Once, after a bhāva darśan, I was lying on the veranda of the hut in front of the *kaḷari*[1], thinking, "O God, let at least *this* be true! How many places I've wandered in search of God! How many proofs I concocted to establish the non-existence of God! How long can one pretend not to have noticed the atrocities committed in God's name? These days, the very word 'God' induces misgivings. The religious are exploiting people's belief in God to promote their own religion."

The uncle who brought me to see Amma found it hard to take me back with him. My family members had sent me with him because they thought a white discoloration that had suddenly appeared on my lips one day was an omen portending a snakebite. The omen that led to my meeting Amma became a cure for the disease of worldliness. Within a few weeks, the discoloration gradually disappeared.

How can a human being become God? Does God have a body? Is all that we believe in true? The observer in me was ignoring the doubting mind and basking in the sweet memories of Amma's love and compassion.

My *pūrvāśram*[2] was near a wide paddy field. It is about 20 kilometers from Vaḷḷickāvu. I used to sit beneath the *Ilanji* tree and gaze at the paddy field. It was where I used to fly kites when I was

[1] Ancestral shrine where Amma used to give darśan.

[2] Literally 'previous āśram.' Those who have taken the monastic path cut off ties with the life they led before, and refer to their biological family members or the house they lived in before joining the monastery as being part of their

young. I would walk long distances along the ridges in the field to enjoy the beauty of the ears of paddy fluttering in the breeze. Often, when I rode on my bicycle to take in the scenic beauty of nature, the bicycle would slip from the ridges. Whenever I got up from the ground, my clothes dirtied, I would wonder if anyone had noticed.

But after meeting Amma, my outlook changed considerably. I am beginning to see clearly the reflection of Jagadīśvari, the Goddess of the Universe, in the raindrop and the dewdrop. Even if I should tumble into dirty water, I now feel that I am still in Jagadīśvari's lap. How did the first lessons in worship become so pleasing? How did compassion arise for the mice sneaking off with ears of paddy? My fingers are reluctant to pluck flowers even for worshipping God. When I strung the flowers scattered on the ground beneath the Ilanji tree, my grandmother protested. "My dear, how can you offer God the flowers that have fallen to the ground? You must make garlands from flowers plucked from the tree."

The feeling that I should have the attitude of begging the plant's forgiveness for causing it pain by plucking its flowers grew stronger. I stood gazing, transfixed, at the dawning within of every one of Amma's *sankalpas*, proof of her shower of blessings.

If there were no sun, would the moon have any beauty? What lends light and life to the world, and adorns it with colors, are your invisible hands, aren't they? While stringing garlands in the *pūja* room, I was beginning to realize that the glittering drawing of the deity is not just a picture. Even in places where there are no such pictures, I was beginning to feel the invisible consciousness shedding its compassion.

There was a time when I used to think that being strong meant being intellectual. I thought science would be able to conquer the

---

pūrvāśram. Thus, 'pūrvāśram mother' means biological mother (as opposed to spiritual mother).

universe. The idea that science brought about all advances began to disappear.

Once, when I was a small child, I went with my pūrvāśram mother to a Devi temple for a special prayer session. At that time, I used to think that the deities carved on the headstone were living beings. That day, I crawled into the lap of the Devi idol, pretending to drink Her milk, unaware of the crowd that had formed around me, watching me. During my childhood, I had no awareness that it was an idol. Children have the innocence needed for experiencing the rapture of the soul, a bliss that is the culmination of imagination.

However, the change brought about by modern education was huge. I began to doubt the very existence of God. I began to wonder if there was a need for His help. I began to take pride in my own abilities. Schools have become an arena for destroying the innocence of children. I have only now begun to notice the change in my mind. Innocence, simplicity and fearlessness are the hallmarks of omniscience. Amma's beautiful form, which sparkles with signs of omniscience, became clearer and clearer in my mind.

Veṭṭikuḷangara Devi Temple

2

THE VEṬṬIKUḶANGARA KĀTYĀYANI Devi temple was near my pūrvāśram. In my childhood days, I would run to the temple after school. Do you know why? To play in the temple grounds!

No matter how often you fell in those sweet temple grounds, you would never get injured. I didn't know then that those white sands were Amma's lap too. Tired after playing, I would go and sit under the banyan tree in the temple. It was then that I would notice the figurines installed there. People would worship the deities in all the shrines within the temple without understanding the significance of those divine forms. Nevertheless, the faith this worship evoked was great indeed.

My grandmother used to tell me stories of people who had visions of Devi in these very temple grounds. *The Divine Mother won't let even a drunkard who trespasses on the temple property go scot-free.* Whenever she said this, her facial expression would change. I now recall with amazement that the birth-star of the goddess enshrined in the temple is Kārtika, Amma's birth-star. Later experiences proved to me that this was no mere coincidence. Amma must have had certain intentions behind associating me with that temple during my formative years.

Aren't temples a means for the ordinary person to experience the presence of God easily? Amma has said, "Even though there is wind everywhere, we feel it much more under a tree. Coolness is felt more keenly near a fan." Even though God is everywhere, we can experience divinity more clearly in a temple or in the presence of a mahātma.

The spiritually enlightened can infuse *prāṇa śakti* [vital force] even into stones, saturating them with divine consciousness. When the stone submits totally to the sculptor, it becomes an idol. Thereafter, its place is no longer on the stairs, but in the shrine. When the stone that silently bore the stomping, abuse and thrashing of many people while on the staircase reaches the hands of an expert sculptor, it becomes an idol capable of imparting peace to thousands.

Temples where mahātmas install the deities and infuse their prāṇa śakti into the deities are transformed into hallowed places of pilgrimage. If a stone, considered lifeless, can gain the strength to impart peace to hundreds of thousands of people, why can't human beings?

Because of egoism and selfishness. These, Amma says, are what stand in the way as obstacles.

How many thousands of stone-like people Amma has transmuted into embodiments of skilled, selfless, volunteer work, by her mere touch! Ahalya, who was trapped within a stone, was transformed into a beautiful woman by the touch of Lord Rāma's feet[3]. Likewise, how many wonders we have been witness to, thanks to that flow of love, which kindles the beauty of the soul.

My faith in God had begun to wane during my college days. While admiring the wonders of nature, I failed to remember the power behind them. Scientists strive to understand what this universe is. They don't ponder *why* this world is. Spirituality teaches us to ask, "Why this world?" and "Why this life?" There is no way that a world based upon definite laws can be devoid of meaning. This world is humanity's path to wholeness. All our experiences here are a part of our training to reach that ultimate goal. For those who can see the universe as training grounds, the world is the domain of divine experiences.

To use Amma's language, we are here for a picnic. If we give undue importance to this world, we will suffer. Those who cherish worldly things deeply will be shattered if everything they value is lost. We must live with the awareness that everything in this world is perishable. While ascending step-by-step to Wholeness, we leave behind the lower steps. Similarly, we may lose all that we have gained so far.

Amma has discovered the secret of saving humanity from the sorrows of life. It was the same secret Prince Siddhārtha unearthed when he became Lord Buddha. What was it? That in this world, there is no such thing as sorrow! If there is no world, how can sorrow be real?

The experiences caused by the illusion of the world are all unreal. Only the Experiencer is real: the Self, which is witness to everything.

The dream world is real to the dreamer. There is only one way to help a man who is crying because of a nightmare—wake

---

[3] A reference to an incident in the Rāmāyaṇa in which Ahalya is cursed by her husband to take the form of a stone for her infidelity. Later, Lord Rāma releases her from the curse by stepping on the stone.

him up. The dream world becomes unreal to the dreamer who has awakened. Only one who is awake can awaken others.

Amma has come to awaken us, who are suffering under the spell of the dream world. She has entered into our dreams to share our sorrows and to try and awaken us from our slumber. But we are still absorbed in our pleasurable sleep. We can't get enough of it. Pleasures will not satisfy us no matter how much we enjoy them. This implies that we must have experienced a joy greater than that previously.

When a toddler cries, the mother today will put a pacifier in its mouth. It stops crying for some time. When it starts wailing again, she will fill the bottle with milk and put it in the child's hands. After some time, the child starts bawling again, ignoring the milk bottle and toys. This time, the mother will stop the work she is doing and, placing her child on her lap, breastfeed it. The child then stops crying.

If the child had been crying out of hunger, the milk bottle would have sufficed. However, it cannot get the warmth of the mother's bosom and her loving affection from the bottle. The milk bottle will never be enough for the baby who has known the sweetness of breast milk and the bliss of the mother's affectionate cuddling.

Likewise, compared with the bliss of *Brahman* (the Supreme) we enjoyed when we were one with God, material pleasures are nothing. That's precisely why those pleasures become the cause of our disaffection. Nothing less than the experience of God can satisfy us, because we have once experienced fullness.

The desire to enjoy worldly pleasures intensifies our sense of incompleteness. Amma has come to make us aware that we are in fact Whole.

VIMAL

Soul Thirst

3

Everywhere, we can hear the cries of the jīvātma (individual Self) striving to merge with the Paramātma (supreme Self). One who gazes at the setting sun will come to understand the pangs of separation quickly. If we are discerning, we can see this pent-up anguish everywhere in nature.

Every object in the universe is in prayer; only human beings are living with selfish desires. Everyone is seeking God, the very embodiment of bliss. However, people still do not enjoy bliss, even after gaining many objects. Their search for something new continues.

Amma has come as a shower of ambrosia to grant refuge to jīvātmas estranged from the embodiment of bliss, and to infuse strength into them so that they can disentangle themselves from the alluring net of *samsāra*, the cycle of birth and death. However, the vast majority of people are mired in petty pleasures. It seems to me that Amma is taking us back to our childhood, when we could enjoy imagining elephants and horses in the clouds!

We don't notice the wonders surrounding us. There are such marvels everywhere in nature. If we gaze at the millions of stars in the endlessly expansive blue skies, the towering edifices of our egos will come crashing down.

When we stand on the seashore and gaze upon the sea converging with the sky, noting the beautiful play of colors on the horizon and reflecting upon the depth of the ocean, our egos shrivel up. A man standing next to a lofty mountain realizes how puny he is. Likewise, we are reduced to nothing in the presence of a mahātma. The snow-capped mountains of our egos melt into teardrops, becoming a Gangetic flow of devotion that washes away our mental impurities. It is possible to become nothing before Amma. If we can be nothing, we can be everything. Amma is infusing into us the innocence of an ignorant babe. Unlike modern education, which stuffs us only with the ego of knowledge, the heart of one with an attitude of surrender will attain the purity of Lord Kṛshṇa's golden flute. We may not get a better opportunity than this to fulfill the great goal of life—to become the flute that endlessly issues divine music.

All inquiries must cease. Should one still attend college for further studies, knowing the dangers of modern education? When I put this question to Amma, she said, "Son, everything is divine. It's enough if you don't allow knowledge to be the cause of egoism. Materialism and spirituality are not two. What matters most is our attitude. Our body, mind and intellect are only instruments. We must know how to use them sensibly. If we then gain knowledge, we will not be egoistic. Even in material life, we can see clearly how lives that have come into contact with God's powers have been transformed."

Where there is supreme knowledge, there the ego cannot be. The ego is little-informed. The hallmarks of omniscience are simplicity and humility. We can see these divine qualities in Amma at all times.

The knower, the knowing and the known become one. Just as a man who was dreaming realizes upon waking up that the whole dream world existed within him, our outlook changes with the realization that the appearance of the universe comes from within.

The mere presence of a mahātma like Amma is potent enough to bring about wondrous transformations in us. Nothing that happens in life is a coincidence. It's said that there are specific reasons for everything. The fact that I felt a bond of many lifetimes with Amma when I first saw her indicates many unknown factors.

I recall an incident that took place when I was one. It's uncommon for anyone to remember anything that happened before the age of two, but this unusual occurrence has remained indelible in my memory. It's as clear as something that happened yesterday.

My pūrvāśram mother was trying to rock me to sleep in my crib. She then walked away to the kitchen. Actually, I hadn't fallen asleep. After my mother had left, I opened my eyes. Not seeing my mother, I peered through the slats of the crib. I saw a woman garbed in pure white and wearing ornaments, her whole body dazzling, walking toward me. She came to my crib and began caressing me gently, showering love on me. Seeing that unfamiliar form, I became frightened and started bawling. Hearing my cries, my mother ran from the kitchen. By then, I had fainted. Seeing me unconscious and motionless, she sprinkled water on my face and tried to revive me.

A short while later, I opened my eyes. This incident continued to take place every day. Many doctors examined me. None was able to diagnose the cause of my fainting spells. Finally, my father went to an astrologer. Using cowry shells[4], he gained some insights that he shared with my father. He said that I was in the presence of a

[4] Some astrologers use cowry shells as a means of divination.

divine being, and that this was conducive to my own well-being. He assured my father that there was no need for any expiatory rites. He also instructed my father to make me wear a silver bangle consecrated at the Ettumānūr temple in order to ward off my fear. As soon as the silver bangle was put on my hand, I stopped noticing the divine visitations.

I did not see that form again until the age of 14 when the experience recurred. I was a high school student then. Since that time, I have lain for hours without any control over my body, undergoing every one of the experiences that happen at the time of death. Over time, those divine experiences that unveiled unknown spheres of life became natural to me.

These experiences fuelled my search for God. The divine visitations inspired me to learn more about extra-sensory powers. It increased my desire to know more about the secrets of life that lie behind what one can see and hear.

My search brought me to the holy presence of Amma, the Goddess of the Universe. When I imbibed Amma's divine love, the seeker in me disappeared.

It was while I was a student of engineering that I got the opportunity to learn more about extra-sensory powers. Accompanied by my rationalist friends, I went to various places. Sites that were supposed to be inhabited by ghosts and ghouls, haunted houses, the abodes of so-called saints with claims to divine power—I went personally to all these places and strove hard to find out the truth for myself.

What I understood was that spirits and ghosts were not as dangerous as human beings! People's faith gets exploited everywhere.

When I met Amma, I didn't forget to ask her the questions that arose in my mind. However, it only dawned on me later that I was putting questions to a divine incarnation.

"Amma, I would like to clear many doubts. May I ask some questions?"

When she heard my request, Amma smiled and said, "But Amma knows nothing! Go ahead, son, ask. Amma will just mutter some rubbish."

"Amma, does God exist?"

Swift was her reply. "Son, isn't that a foolish question? Asking if God exists is like asking, 'Do I have a tongue?' with your own tongue. Why are you asking now, son?"

"If God does exist, I've enough anger in me to kill Him!"

When she heard my reply, Amma laughed loudly and asked, "Why, son?"

I explained why I was angry with God. "So many people in the world are suffering because of disease and poverty. Some are living in the lap of luxury. Creation is such that every creature in this world is food for another. I'm furious with the God who created this cruel universe."

Amma responded, as if agreeing with my criticism, "Amma likes you, son. You're not angry with God for any selfish reason, but out of compassion for others. God dwells in hearts that feel compassion for others. He is not someone who punishes. He protects everyone. We are the ones who are punishing ourselves. All our deeds are recorded in nature. We must experience their consequences in this life or in the coming ones. If we live like animals after having gained a human body, we may be reborn as animals, or become food for another animal. God cannot be blamed for this."

"Amma, are you God?"

Amma laughed and said, "Son, Amma is a crazy girl. No one has jailed her. That's why she's still here. Son, Amma is not telling you to believe in her or in a God who dwells in the sky. It's enough if you believe in yourself. Everything is in you. Like the colossal tree waiting to emerge from the seed, divine power pervades the whole universe. If one awakens that divine power through prayer, meditation and good deeds, one can attain Fullness. One can merge in God, and thus transcend birth and death. The vault containing the secrets of the universe will open. In that state of being, one will behold God in all creatures, moving and unmoving. Seeing God in all, one will gain the purity to love and serve. This is the supreme state a human being can attain."

Amma slowly closed her eyes. I gazed at that face radiating the rapture of Brahman. When I beheld the infinite glories of God in Amma, I was unable to ask anything else.

Mahātmas incarnate in order to teach the world how a human being can attain Fullness. Amma's life proves that nothing, not even being born into the most unfavorable of circumstances, is an obstacle to God-realization.

It became clear to me that nothing in life is accidental. We must acquire the mental purity to understand the meaning behind every incident in life. There are definite purposes behind Amma's life. She must have taken the necessary steps to prepare for these purposes long before. I also began to understand that Amma had already taken steps long before to protect us from getting ruined by the clutches of samsāra. The sense that I had been given a new life began to grow in me. The rest of my life is a return trip to childhood. Teardrops are witness to the truth that Amma's divine presence is enough to awaken the lost innocence.

Paranormal Powers

4

Above, the endless, expansive sky! What an enchanting universe, with planets and satellites revolving around blazing, twinkling stars! The sky, sea, mountains, vales, birds, beasts, flowers and trees intoxicate us with their colorful beauty. Who is behind nature's magic? How did all these things come into being? Did God create them?

When scientists strive to learn about universal phenomena, they realize the limitations of the mind and intellect. The more they learn, the more they realize how abysmal their ignorance is. The champions of intellectual power, unable to unveil the most hidden secrets of creation, get baffled. The *ṛshis* [seers] never inquired into *what* this universe is, rather *why*.

This universe is God's means for taking humanity to Fullness. It is a treasure trove of wonders, bestowing myriad experiences commensurate with people's varying levels of maturity and understanding.

Everyone lives in his or her own world. It is the human mind that creates heaven and hell.

Experiences are changing continuously. All experiences are unreal, only the Experiencer is real. When that Experiencer becomes known, everything else will disappear; the Truth will be realized. The awareness encompassed by the scriptural dictum '*Brahma satyam, jagan mithya*' ['Brahman alone is true, the world is illusory'] will dawn. God has given us this life so that we may attain this awareness.

Nothing can be rejected. Instead, we must develop the expansiveness of heart to embrace everything. This is what Amma is showing us—the ability to see only the good. Through the *bhāva* [divine mood] of the Mother, Amma is giving us the gift of inner purity with which we can overcome the perversities of the mind and attain the divine experience of eternal beauty, thus fulfilling our lives.

Before meeting Amma, I cried numberless times for no reason, sitting in solitude! In the last watches of moonlit nights, my mind would yearn for *something.* Amma, the *antaryāmi* [indweller], must have been trying, even then, to console me. Today, I know it was her hands that came in the form of the cool breeze to wipe away my tears.

When one meets a mahātma like Amma, the mind begins to turn inward. There will come a moment when our bond with the outer world gets severed. Such moments are powerful life experiences of great significance, for our very individuality is turned upside down. Others will begin to see us anew.

I recall a visit to a haunted house in northern Kerala. At my friend's request, we decided to conduct some investigations there. We saw inauspicious omens right at the threshold of the uninhabited house: a cobra slithering down the steps to the pool, cobwebs covering the house's exterior, the sounds of bats flapping their wings—these alone were enough to make the atmosphere terrifying, never mind the ghosts!

My friend and I sat down on the veranda of the locked house. I looked over the grounds. Even during sunrise and sunset, the sun's rays would pass, seemingly without touching this south-facing house, half of which had been hacked away. We learned that many people had died in the pool there. That's why no one had bothered even to clean the place for years.

At dusk, the night sentry arrived with a lantern. I asked him, "Don't you ever feel frightened staying here alone?"

"Sir, would getting scared help? I must survive, mustn't I?" he said with a sigh. "I can't remember the last time I slept with my wife and kids. I was no longer healthy enough to do other jobs. That's when I got this offer, which no one else dared to accept."

We listened to his ghost stories and laughed. He said that he wore metal-foil amulets—which were inscribed with mantras and which had been consecrated at a temple—on both hands and around his neck to ward off evil spirits. Therefore, he had no fear. I reflected upon the courage that innocent faith can give a person.

The problem isn't whether or not God exists, but whether believing in God is of any benefit. A metal-foil inscribed with mantras making one fearless—it is this sense of security that the modern man and woman lack. And this is why our fears are growing. Fears make us look upon everything with suspicion. With nothing to comfort a mind that has no faith in anything, we begin running after mirages in the desert of life. Unable to find the spring within, we roam about, trying to quench our thirst.

Even though we had to put up with the disquieting sounds of bats flying about and dogs howling, we spent a few days there waiting for the ghosts. We didn't learn anything about paranormal powers. We left, concluding that the whole thing—ghosts, spirits and all—was a figment of people's subconscious minds.

I learned later that many of the so-called haunted houses had been built in violation of the laws of *vāstu śāstra*[5]. There is no doubt that having a *tuḷasi* altar in the courtyard and a lamp-lit prayer room in clear view will change the very appearance of the house's premises. We must be careful about adorning walls with disfigured images or the severed heads of animals. Every object exerts an influence on the mind. We should not try to cram our homes with unnecessary objects. When we step into a house adorned with neatly and methodically arranged pictures that invoke the remembrance of God, and with objects that have a revitalizing presence, we can feel our minds quieten.

We can experience peace in Amma's presence, no matter where she is. They say it's impossible to put mahātmas in hell; put them there, and hell becomes heaven! Until I reached the lotus feet of Amma, by whose very presence everyone can enjoy the bliss of heaven, I continued my search for paranormal powers.

I visited shrines featuring deities with fearsome forms. These deities had been installed for the sole purpose of destroying enemies. Such places exploit people's weaknesses in order to make money. Afterward, I realized that the significance of pūjas for destroying one's enemies is not that the enemies are killed, but that the feeling of enmity is. When adversaries turn into allies, when hatred is transformed into love, when anger becomes compassion, the attitude of enmity is killed. Before this can happen, we must abandon all likes and dislikes. Divine qualities should be revived in the cool air of love.

Any action done with the aim of harming others will be the cause of our own ruin. Thoughts of hatred issue from us like arrows, zoom toward the intended target, hit that person and whiz

---

[5] The Indian science concerned with the positioning of objects in order to harness the flow of positive energy and divert the flow of negative energy. Similar to Feng Shui.

back toward us as a curse that is 10 times as powerful. This is why there are so many stories illustrating how the creators of terrifying deities that destroy enemies had to endure miseries for many generations. Kindly thoughts will benefit others, then return as a shower of blessings that are similarly magnified.

I remember the festivals celebrated in the ancestral temple of my pūrvāśram family. I was a student then. All the family members would gather for the celebrations. As part of the festivities, *kaḷamezhuttu* songs[6] would be sung to propitiate the *nāga* [serpent] gods.

Young girls were arrayed before the kaḷamezhuttu, drawn before the shrines of the nāga *yakshi* [demigoddess] and nāga king deities. Minstrels began singing hymns to propitiate these deities. The euphonious sounds of the accompanying musical instruments and boisterous roars from devotees created an intoxicating atmosphere. "What's all this about?" I asked my father. A welcome for the nāga yakshi and nāga king, he said. Hearing my father's explanation, I surveyed the scene eagerly. The drum beats and ululations[7] reached a crescendo. The hollering became more intense. The girls, who had hitherto been sitting with bowed heads, started behaving differently. People could sense the presence of the nāga deities in these girls who held stalks of flowers. They began swaying, like serpents. Their gaze and the movements of their limbs bore striking similarities to the swaying of a snake. These girls moved hypnotically from side to side, swaying to the music. The devotees started shouting in total abandon. Even after the predetermined duration of the function was over, the girls continued dancing. All attempts to restrain them proved futile. No matter how hard they tried, people were just not able to subdue the girls. How did these young girls become so strong? The music stopped. As the

[6] Kaḷamezhuttu refers to decorative pictures of deities drawn on the floor with colored powder. The songs mentioned here are about these deities.

[7] Traditionally, women hoot in shrill voices during auspicious occasions.

priest sprinkled consecrated water on them, the girls slithered to the threshold of the shrine. There, they prostrated, then remained prostrate, motionless.

What had happened to those girls? How can the soul of a snake enter a human body? What is the essence of nāga worship? I didn't have answers to these questions then, but I couldn't ignore the fact that many of the beliefs I had dismissed as blind were a consolation to people.

I learned from Amma that if we arouse the *kuṇḍalini śakti* [serpent power] lying dormant in the *mūlādhāra cakra*, we will enjoy many divine experiences. We are attempting to stir that divine power through the worship of God, which awakens the divine qualities within. When the limitless power that resides in our mūlādhāra cakra, personified as Kanyākumāri, becomes one with Parameśvara, who resides in the *sahasrāra cakra* in Kailāsh, we will realize the Truth, the essence of spiritual fulfilment[8]. In that divine experience, when one gets bathed in the nectar of immortality, one transcends all sense of individuality.

God is devoid of names and forms, but all names are His; all forms too. Our spiritual experiences are based on our faith and ideas about God. No matter what our concept of God may be, validating it is no problem for the Almighty. Devotees have different experiences, based on the diverse ideas they have of divinity. We can fill the vessel of our minds with divine energy. The shape of that vessel is not important; we have the freedom to choose the vessel we like. When we take the path of devotion, worship of God becomes more and more gratifying. The zeal for attaining

[8] The process of spiritual evolution is likened to the legend of Kanyākumāri. According to the story, Kanyākumāri, the Virgin Goddess, is waiting at India's southern tip for Parameśvara (Lord Śiva), who resides in the Himālayan abode of Mount Kailash, in Indian's northern-most region. Their union symbolizes the culmination of spiritual evolution.

oneness with our *ishṭa devata* (preferred form of divinity) causes our *vāsanas* (latent tendencies) to wither.

It's difficult to feel enthused about a God one hasn't seen, but it's easy to perceive all the deities in a Satguru. Therefore, when we develop unshakable devotion for and faith in the Satguru, divine experiences that we may have thought unattainable come in search of us. That's why there is no need for those who have reached a Satguru to worship other deities. An exalted disciple will be able to perceive the different aspects of all the 33 *crore* deities in a Guru[9].

I once visited the home of a woman who used to cry daily after her son died. The son's soul, it seems, would possess the mother's body. During that time, her voice would change. Even her very nature would change. Her style of speaking and behavior would be like that of a man. I noted this unusual change in her demeanor. That woman, whose health had become weakened by sorrow, moved here and there with the vigor of an athlete.

The untimely death of her son, who had been a sportsman, had broken the mother's heart. After his death, she would sometimes act like her son. That day, she proclaimed loudly but indistinctly that she was the son who had come to see his mother. After some time, she asked for some drinking water. When water was poured into her mouth, she started gulping it eagerly. She then closed her eyes. When some water was sprinkled on her face, she opened her eyes again, and started staring at those present. She seemed to have become normal again. Why had everyone gathered around her, she asked? It was clear that she did not remember anything that had just happened.

How did such a thing occur? It's proof that the son, though dead, continues to live in his mother's heart. This experience—that

[9] Hindus believe that there are a total of 33 crore [330 million] deities. This may be interpreted as meaning that the one indivisible Godhead can take on an infinite number of forms.

her son hadn't died but was continuing to live as part of her being—was a great relief to her. The mother's subconscious mind knew her son's habits and actions very well. The mother's heart, which lacked the strength to accept the truth that her son had died, strove to make him live through her. This was the conclusion my intellect drew. That woman hadn't been acting; she had been identified with her son's personality. Even death cannot sever that bond of love. I will always remember this truth, that the dead continue living in the hearts of those who love them.

Enlightened souls can identify with any divine bhāva. These infinite divine bhāvas are in us all, but an ordinary human can manifest only human or demonic bhāvas, whereas a Satguru like Amma can identify herself with any divine bhāva. There was a time when I used to scrutinize Amma closely during her bhāva darśans. The Guru may play along with the foolishness of someone who, even after reaching Her, tries to evaluate the Guru through the intellect. I too tried to measure the infinity that is Amma with the limited yardstick of my intellect. Amma, the embodiment of compassion, looked upon my actions as those of an ignorant child, laughing blissfully at my foibles. When the son wrestles with his father, the father doesn't mind admitting defeat. Not only that, he won't forget to praise his son for his strength too! A father acts in this way to make his son happy. Similarly, Amma continued to encourage me for as long as I tried to size her up intellectually.

Dusshāsana, who tried to disrobe Draupadi, finally collapsed, exhausted[10]. Until I too fell, exhausted by my attempts to unravel the Truth with intellectual tactics, Amma waited patiently and compassionately.

---

[10] In the Mahābhārata, Duryodhana orders Dusshāsana to disrobe Draupadi publicly to humiliate her. In utter helplessness, she calls out to Lord Kṛshṇa, whose grace causes the sari she is wearing to become an endless ream of cloth.

In the Bower of the Heart

5

There is music even in silence. There is dance even in stillness. There is beauty even in ugliness. There is the coolness of bliss even in the heat of sorrow. We can experience all these when divine love awakens. They were the first lessons I learned in Amma's sacred presence. "Son, how can we reject anything? We should know how to enjoy life. We should submit to God so that He can correct the ideas we have been harboring. We need to have an attitude of surrender. The concepts our minds have cherished should be erased."

We don't notice the presence of fireflies in sunlight. Candlelight isn't necessary then. The dawn of wisdom dispels all phenomenal experiences. Amma is that sun of knowledge. She is the stream of compassion that takes us from the shadows of individuality to the luminous tower of totality.

Amma was the answer to all my doubts. She was also the proof for all answers. In Amma's presence, logic and intellect vanish. The Himālayan layers of my ego melted in tears that washed her holy feet.

My life was becoming a return trip to my lost childhood. The days that followed ushered me into the awareness that childhood is not a state that only those from a certain age group can experience. All those who reach Amma's presence realize that people of any age can experience the sweetness of childhood. This becomes apparent in the moments we pledge our egos to the God or the Guru. I didn't realize that Amma's nearness was making me a child. The mesmerizing might of her motherliness bred the feeling that we were toddling infants. The flow of Amma's love and compassion was dissolving me into a non-entity. I perceived new meanings in everything I saw and heard.

* * *

The *Taipuyam*[11] festival in Harippāḍ temple—thousands thronged the temple and the streets to watch the *kāvaḍi* dance. Many devotees who have taken religious vows carry the kāvaḍi as an offering to Lord Muruga. Many danced to the beat of drums and music. How splendid was the sight of a thousand peacock feathers moving in tandem! The flock of devotees danced in abandon, symbols of an innocence devoid of artificiality. They were not dancing for anyone or for any kind of reward. The intoxication of devotion culminates in dance. The first sight of these dancers made it clear that they were not paid dancers or inebriated by alcohol. For these devotees who had been observing all aspects of the vow for days, worshipping Lord Muruga and begging for alms with the intention of forsaking all sense of personal pride and honor, and ready to

[11] The day of pūyam (pushyam), the eighth lunar asterism, in the month of Tai. This day is traditionally dedicated to Lord Muruga. Votaries carry a kāvaḍi [decorated arched pole], adorned with peacock feathers to propitiate Muruga. Many kāvaḍi bearers dance. Some pierce their bodies with spears or tridents. Some, as part of their vow, walk on a bed of burning coals.

surrender even bodily awareness to God, these were indescribably blissful moments. They were pure souls who had forgotten the material world, if only temporarily, and were moving to the rhythm of the cosmic dance. These devotees were transfigured into Lord Muruga's colorful vehicle.

Such festivals are opportunities to encounter the sacred experience of being transformed into carriers of the divine. In order to become vehicles for the divine, our hearts should become hallowed shrines. As Lord Kṛshṇa told Arjuna, the body is a temple. Amma reminds us that when our hearts become temples, we will experience divinity within. Amma is striving to turn us all into mobile temples. We must become carriers of the divine, capable of spreading peace throughout the world. Even those mired in sensual pleasures can attain innocence and purity of devotion through vows. The tridents that pierce the skin do not hurt these devotees. They don't get burnt while walking on a bed of burning coals. The reason is that their minds are on God. At that time, the natural elements do not strew their path with obstacles. Śankarācārya's disciple, who forgot everything else when he heard the call of the Guru, just walked across the river; lotus petals sprang up to support his feet[12]. Nature cannot but help those who lose themselves in the remembrance of God. The moments in which we forget, briefly at least, our identification with the body, mind and intellect, yield wondrous experiences.

"Son, is anything impossible for one who has nullified the ego?" Amma's words aren't borrowed from anyone. They flow like ambrosia from the throne of omniscience in which she is ensconced. Amma is the divine presence that makes even questions about God seem irrelevant. "Is there anything that isn't God?" Not everyone may understand these words of Amma. An ordinary person may transcend the realm of the body, mind and intellect

[12] This disciple came to be known as Padmapāda (literally, lotus-footed).

partially or fully when she forgets her individuality. A man dreaming of his beloved won't notice someone walking in front of him. A maidservant thinking of her baby whom she has left sleeping in her house will not notice if her clothes catch fire. There are times in the life of ordinary people when their sense organs stop functioning without their knowledge, but they cannot sustain this state. When the activities of the mind cease, the realms of divine experiences within get activated.

Once, while I was in Amma's presence during Devi Bhāva, I noticed a group of people from Tamil Nāḍu dancing and laughing raucously. They were moving fast, with closed eyes, their bodies coming close together as they danced. The dance was so vigorous that if the dancers had collided during the dance, they would have been done for! But the fact that they never knocked into each other, though dancing with eyes closed, amazed me. Later, I learned that they had taken the vow of dancing through fire at the shrine of Māḍan in Kollam. I also learned that they would only proceed for the fire dance after obtaining permission from Amma. I asked them why they sought her permission. They said that whenever they had danced without Amma's permission, they had been burnt. These devotees, who had come to seek her permission, were now dancing in total abandon. They were dancing at frightening speed, laughing boisterously all the while. I didn't understanding the meaning of this laughing dance. I asked Amma.

She said, "Son, they may see God as a lover of strident laughter. Uncontrollable bliss may culminate in such laughter. This then becomes a dance."

When words prove insufficient to express the emotions of the mind, they manifest as dance. When we get angry, our gesticulations change, our gaze changes, our movements change, our rate of breathing changes, our facial expression changes—they become dancerly. When we feel love, there is a change in the movements of our limbs. Our gesticulations and facial expressions change totally and get transmuted into dance. The bliss of divine experience transforms us into dancers.

We can alter life according to our ideas. We can realize the God of our imagination. We can be anything we want, but the right ideas should first sprout in our minds.

We can attain Fullness in this very life itself. Amma is showing us the ways to do so through her life. The sacrifices she has undergone to lead us from the dense jungle of the intellect to the shady bower of the heart are indescribable tales. Why squander this human life? Why remain confined only within the straitjacket of our bodies, minds and intellects? We must regard this sacred life as an opportunity to break open the imprisoning cage of attachments and soar into indestructibility. Amma is constantly working to awaken divine qualities within us through her compassion-filled gaze, consoling touch and ambrosial utterances. Life becomes beautiful when we change our outlooks.

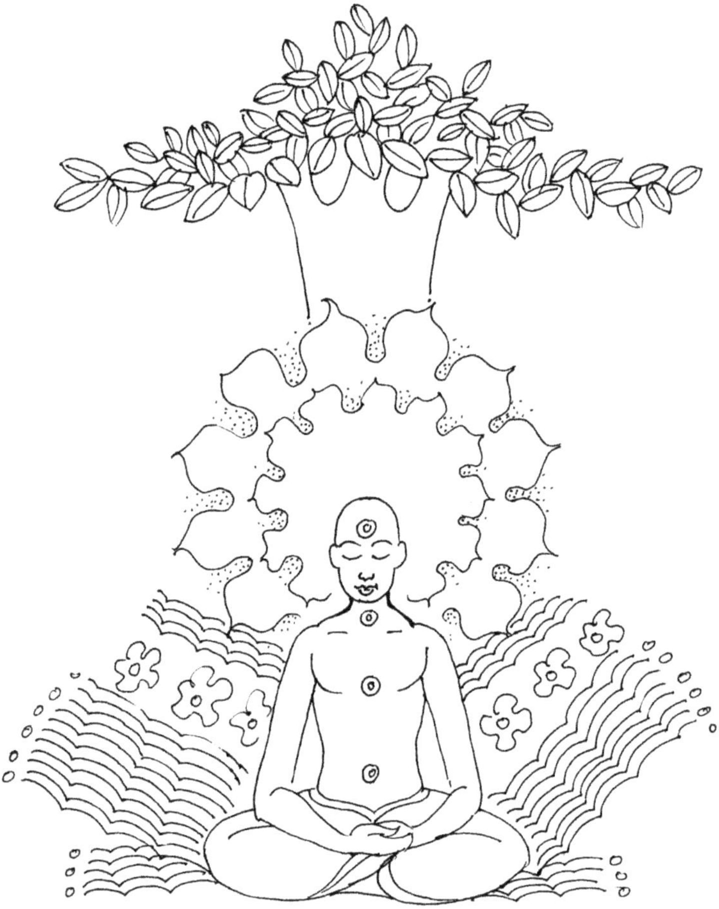

The Sun of Knowledge

6

Night's inky blackness flees with sunrise. The atmosphere of fear that darkness creates is dispelled. All misgivings disappear. The sun's rays infuse all beings with renewed vitality. Similar is the change that the dawning within of Amma, the sun of knowledge, creates.

More alarming than night is darkness bred from ignorance. The mind can create the illusion of something that doesn't exist. This thinking is also the cause of our ignorance about all that does exist.

If we try to learn only about the outer world and not about ourselves, we won't be able to understand reality. All that we see and hear are merely projections of our own conceptions.

A man standing forlorn amid people speaking in unfamiliar languages felt reassured when he heard the sound of his own language. When someone explained what the others had been talking about, his facial expression changed; although he wasn't aware of it, a smile dawned slowly on his face.

That poor man had thought the others were making fun of him. He only realized that they had been praising him when someone who knew his language came forward to patiently explain matters to him. He realized that he had wasted time feeling sorry for himself when he ought to have been rejoicing.

It is our great fortune that we have a *mahāguru* [great Guru] with us in the form of a Mother to dispel similar misconceptions of life.

> *karayunnatiniyentinakhilēśi tirupādattaṇaññennatariññillayō*
> Why are you crying? Don't you know you have reached near the Holy Feet of the Goddess of the Universe?
>
> from the bhajan *'Akalattākōvilil'*

Keep in mind these lines. However, even after having Amma's darśan, enemies in the form of likes and dislikes may become the cause of sorrowful experiences. Still, we can destroy them through discrimination.

I recall an incident that happened before I became an āśram resident. During one of the bhāva darśan days, I didn't get a chance to speak to Amma. Feeling dejected, I sat in a corner of the grounds in front of the kaḷari. Dawn was approaching. Although bhāva darśan had ended, Amma hadn't gone to sleep yet. Many devotees in front of the kaḷari surrounded her. Some people had the impression that as soon as bhāva darśan was over, Amma would revert to being a child. She was never shy about singing loudly, joking or even wrestling with devotees. Amma knew how to be like a child in front of those who saw her as one. She also knew how to be Devi in front of those who saw her as the Goddess. Maybe these *līlās* were necessary to teach us that Amma could be anything she wanted. In her presence, just how much bliss people were experiencing was eloquently expressed by their facial expressions. Those who had to leave by the 5:00 a.m. bus wouldn't leave Amma. They had become embodiments of innocence, totally unaware of time or place. They were singing and dancing with Amma.

Amma got up from that place all of a sudden. She ran to where I was seated. Sitting down on the ground next to me, she asked, "Son, why are you sitting alone? Don't you want Amma? Have you become strong enough to sit all alone? Solitude is good, son. You must enjoy the experience of solitude." Cradling my head on her shoulders, She sang,

enne marannu ñān ennilūṭennoru tankakkināvil layiccu
koṭiyabdhangaḷ pinniṭṭa kathakaḷen cārusirayiludiccuyarnnu
annutoṭṭanyamāyi kāṇan kazhiññilla ellām
entātmāvennōrttu

Forgetting myself, I merged in a golden dream that arose from within me.
The events of millions of years gone by rose up within me.
From that day onward, I was unable to perceive anything as different or separate from my own inner Self;
everything was a single unity.

from the bhajan '*Ānandavīthiyil*'

Amma said, "Son, when you've known the bliss of solitude, you won't have the sense of otherness anymore." '*From that day onward, I was unable to perceive anything as different or separate from my own inner Self; everything was a single unity.*' —Amma sang that line again and again.

Those who have become one with nature, those who know that they have dissolved in the ocean of Brahman, don't have any sense of 'other.' Everything is theirs. They see their own Self everywhere.

Solitude doesn't mean aloneness. The thought that we are alone gives rise to sorrow. It makes one alarmed. It destroys self-confidence. It breeds anxiety and fills life with miseries. However, solitude isn't like that. It's a state of union with God. It is filled with the priceless moments of sharing one's heart with God. Where is the place that we can be alone? When God permeates every place, there is no meaning in even thinking that we're alone. We must be able to relish solitude.

Life is a rush. Where is the time for solitude if we are entangled in the mesh of attachments? Material life becomes a prison. If we remain there, how can we know the beauty of the golden dawn of eternal freedom? That's why Amma says, "Children, become free. Understand that life at present is enslavement. Change the ideas you have hitherto cherished."

An elephant that has been trapped submits at last to its trainers. After its training, it won't try to break free, even if its enclosure is made from twigs. There's no one to tell it that it is imprisoned in a cage of twigs. Imagining itself to be fenced in by iron, the elephant tries to reconcile itself to the prison. We are imprisoned in a cage that's even flimsier than the twig enclosure. However, neither a sensualist nor the indolent can break free. Only the brave can. If we can break loose from this jail, all the notions we have been harboring will be obliterated. Life will become a playground for experiencing boundless bliss.

Through practice, we can remain alone even amid a madding crowd. We must train the mind. When we can see the Self in everything, the sense of the 'other' will start vanishing.

We must infuse ourselves with strength instead of dissipating it. We must become a storehouse of energy. When the light of the Self begins to overflow, the feeling that one's own Self has filled everything will arise. Let us cherish Amma's advice: "Don't fritter away your energy in scolding others or grieving."

We should imbibe the bliss of solitude instead of brooding in seclusion. When we surrender our pains to the Lord, even our tears of sorrow will be sweet. We must be careful not to identify with the rain clouds of our sorrows. These clouds are fleeting. How can the clouds of our weak thoughts obscure the sun of our Self? The idea that the clouds are obscuring the sun is a mere fancy. Compared with the size of the sun, how puny the clouds are! Just a puff is enough to scatter the clouds of weakness! To us, the clouds seem to obscure the sun. However, they are actually obscuring our vision, not the sun. We should open the eye that cannot be occluded by Māyā's veil, the eye of knowledge!

Amma has come to open our eye of knowledge. In return, she accepts the burdens of our sins. For the mahātmas who embody compassion, even samsāra is like a playfield.

The journey to the Self is like the scaling of a mountain. Since it is an expedition to the summit, we should discard unnecessary burdens, otherwise the journey will be tough. The lighter the load, the easier the journey.

In truth, nothing that we are carrying around is necessary. We are like the lunatic who stuffs the heap of refuse into sacks and lugs them up the mountain. Fatigued and unable to complete the journey, we will eventually submit to death.

We can lay down at Amma's feet the burden of karmic debts that we have been carrying over lifetimes. The barriers of selfishness collapse in her presence, which the cosmic power has evoked in order to liberate millions of lives. The sorrows of samsāra dissolve in the marvel of universal motherhood.

The world is sustained by the enchanting power of love. Where there is love, there is no distance. If there is love, even language becomes superfluous. Silence is the language of the *Ātma*, the soul. The Ganges of Love cascades from the plane of the Ātma. Words are powerless to define what silence can impart. In the olden days, Guru and disciples communed in silence. They had attained a state wherein they could understand everything without speaking. This is possible at the pinnacle of love. The mother knows what her hungry child needs even before its face becomes wan.

I had been unable to grasp from words or books the wisdom Amma transmitted through this silence during the early days, after I reached her presence. I learned that if we are watchful, we will realize how great are the changes that occur in our minds because of changes in Amma's facial expressions. Her single glance has more power than a thousand words. What cannot be taught? *That* is what the Guru teaches!

Amma was teaching even in her days of absorption in silent meditation. She is always trying to unite human hearts through supreme love. The Guru's shower of grace falls on the disciple who has an attitude of love and surrender. It was through this attitude of surrender that Ekalavya appropriated the lessons of archery from Droṇācārya[13]. Where there is love, there is surrender. A *jñāni*, knower of the supreme truth, is in love with the universe. How can someone who experiences everything in herself not love? When the child Kṛshṇa opened His mouth to reveal the whole universe, Yashoda fell into a swoon. Although her children do not have the mental strength to withstand the cosmic vision, Amma has come prepared to make us understand everything through her motherly affection.

[13] According to the story in the Mahābhārata, Droṇācārya, a master archer, had refused to teach Ekalavya archery when the latter approached him for instruction. But Ekalavya learned covertly, by watching Droṇācārya in secret and then practicing in front of an effigy of Droṇācārya. When Droṇācārya learns about it, he demands his Guru dakshiṇa (honorarium)—Ekalavya's thumb. In the spirit of true surrender to the Guru, Ekalvya cuts off his thumb joyfully and gives it to Droṇācārya, even though he knows that doing so will disable him from practicing archery ever again.

Every single thought in our mind is capable of influencing nature greatly. Therefore, it is an offence to pollute nature with evil thoughts.

"*Manaḥ kṛtam kṛtam rāma, na sarīra kṛtam kṛtam*" says Sage Vaśishṭha in *Yoga Vaśishṭha.* What the mind does is an act, not what the body does. In other words, an action is considered an action only if the mind is behind that action. However, even if we act only with the mind and not with the body, we may still reap the fruits of that action, even if we did not do it physically.

Amma cautions us to handle the instrument of the mind very carefully. The way people handle the mind is similar to the case of a child who has been handed a burning torch. Using the mind without understanding its secrets can cause total destruction.

This is why the Guru gives us a mantra, so that we can tame the mind. Chanting the mantra is a means of cleansing the flow of thoughts. It's not easy to do away with thoughts altogether, but we can use good thoughts to weaken and gradually stop other thoughts totally. As Amma says, if we continue pouring fresh water into a pot of salt water, its salinity will gradually decrease. So, we must fill our minds with noble thoughts. We will then be able to attain inner purity very quickly.

In Love with Nature

7

In India, worship is nothing but a training to make people fall in love with nature. We can still experience the phenomenon of every object in nature fulfilling people's innocent sankalpas (resolves).

I recall an incident that took place when I was in the fourth grade. I was staying in the ancestral home of my pūrvāśram mother. It was within walking distance from my school. I used to enjoy the ambles through the sugarcane fields and byways. When I reached home for lunch, my grandmother said, "Son, after lunch, you must go to the nāga temple. Your uncle is waiting there." It was only then that I remembered the festival at our family temple. Grandmother was particular that all family members should participate in the worship.

I ran down the flight of stone steps in front of the house. Running comes naturally to children, who find speed, and not leisureliness, agreeable. Fatigue is a stranger to children, in whom enthusiasm is apparent in every movement. While running to the temple, I felt I had stepped on something rubbery. I turned around to look. It was a cobra with an upraised hood! Frightened, I ran behind a tree and watched. It slowly glided forward until it reached the path I had to take, where it remained. How could I take that path now? I realized that running had been a bad idea. I told myself that I shouldn't have taken a shortcut when there was a wide road I could have taken. I returned home thinking about the snake that hadn't bitten me even though I had stepped on it. When I reached the gate, I saw my grandmother waiting for me. As soon as she saw me, my grandmother laughed and said, "I knew you would come. I prayed to the snake gods."

"Why?" I asked in amazement.

"I forgot to give you the coconut that was to be given as an offering at the temple. So I prayed to the snake gods to make you come back." When I told her about how I had stepped on a snake, my grandmother laughed. "Don't worry, my boy. The snake gods won't harm you." She put a coconut in a bag and gave it to me. "My child, you must offer this coconut at the shrine of the snake gods."

Apparently, once, my grandmother had felt sad when the cluster of flowers on the coconut tree hadn't ripened into fruits. She had vowed then: "If this coconut tree bears fruit, I shall offer the first bunch of coconuts to the snake gods." However, my uncles, who didn't know anything about this vow, lopped off all the coconuts from the tree so that they could drink coconut water. Even my poor grandmother forgot about the vow! The next time this tree yielded coconuts, they looked like snakes! People gathered to see the coconuts, which resembled the upraised hoods of snakes. All the coconuts were offered at the shrine of the snake gods. As a token of her repentance, my grandmother vowed to offer one coconut every year thereafter. It was the coconut for that year that my grandmother passed me.

At that tender age, I didn't reflect upon the meaning of these incidents. It's not difficult just to accept that *things are like this*—there is no room for doubt at that age. However, questions arise when the intellect develops. The explanation for such experiences, which only those who have fathomed the mysteries of the cosmic mind can give, seemed natural then. Later, when I sought answers for these phenomena, I began to accept the fact that there are many phenomena in nature that the intellect cannot understand.

Both moving and unmoving beings (i.e. humans, animals and plants) can understand the vibration of minds in tune with nature. The purity of innocence causes the flowers of the heart to blossom. Amma caresses us with the cool breeze of motherly love so as to infuse us with the fragrance of love. When we realize that Amma's unseen hands are everywhere in the universe, we develop self-confidence.

Amma says that anything can be accomplished through innocent sankalpas. Such innocence is innate to a jñāni. Even though the innocence of a child and that of a jñāni may look alike, the cause of a child's innocence is ignorance whereas that of a jñāni's is omniscience.

The beauty of ignorance in a child and the beauty of wisdom in a jñāni make each a center of attraction. The sight of even the young of a wild animal evokes feelings of tender affection in everyone. Who else but a jñāni like Amma can be a child and the universal mother simultaneously?

Even though we can discern various facets of Amma—like the confidence to be anyone she wants, fearlessness, a sense of humor, and the humble attitude of knowing nothing—she herself weaves the veils of Māyā that prevent others from understanding *what* Amma is. Sometimes, I recall the days when I used to wander about, unaware that Self-knowledge isn't illumined by the dim light of the intellect.

Cycling was a hobby during my student days. I used to pedal through deserted paddy fields. These excursions became experiences of an entirely different kind after I met Amma. I would stand wonderstruck seeing Amma's affection manifest in every scene of nature. When I saw tiny frogs diving into the water, startled by my bicycle, I couldn't continue cycling along the ridges anymore. Nor did I have the heart to break up the ring of multi-colored birds gleefully circumambulating the patches of fields, adding a spray of hues to the landscape. When I began to realize that everything proclaimed the glory of God, each scene started to fill me with divine joy.

We can never get enough of nature's beauty, no matter how much of it we relish. If we succeed in going with the pristine flow of nature's love, our conceptions of time and space will cease to be. Future and past disappear when we reach the summit of divine love. Time too fades away. Love can thus bring us to the threshold of *samādhi*.

My cycling expeditions through scenes of abundant nature would often end with some problem. Once, I continued cycling until dusk. It was one of those trips undertaken with no idea of where I was heading. Wide paddy fields lay on all four sides. Realizing that I had lost my way and that I had no inkling about where I was, I stopped. I thought of asking someone, but as it was past the usual farming hours, there was no one in that deserted place. I resumed cycling, thinking of riding on until I met someone. I had no idea where I was heading. I did not waste the opportunity to take in the splendor of the night. The silvery clouds seemed to be accompanying me in the moonlight. The fear that I was all alone vanished. Suddenly it happened—the light of the bicycle stopped working! Unable to see my way, I veered round a corner, causing the bicycle to slip. I fell into a small pond. When I saw that the dirty water had dyed my soaked clothes ocher, I felt some joy. Perhaps, this was an omen of some great deed I would do in the future, I thought! I fished the bicycle out, placed it on the ridge and examined it. When I rotated the wheels, I saw that the bulb was working fine. How could I return without washing my clothes? There was no sign of any house nearby. I caught sight of a small temple near where I had fallen. It was closed, as the daily worship had ended. I then noticed a light far away. I walked toward it. Thank God! It was a house! The lamp that had been lit at twilight had not gone out. Seeing a stranger in that unusual garb, the man of the house asked, "What happened? By the looks of it, you must have fallen down in the paddy field." He ushered me into the house and arranged for me to take a bath. After bathing, I sat on the veranda. I was wearing wet clothes; I had washed them because they were dirty.

"My child, people always fall at that particular spot. No one knows why. It's the route the Goddess takes. Nobody crosses that path with a bicycle. Those who have tried to do so always fall." The man smiled and continued, "You probably didn't dismount from your bicycle at that spot."

The woman of the house came out with a cup of coffee and said, "Have a cup of hot coffee."

As I accepted the cup, I thought, "This is truly amazing! Amma has entrusted people everywhere with expressing love." I recalled her immortal words: "Children, don't think Amma is confined to this body."

There must have been an invisible power that inspired this couple to express so much love and kindness to a total stranger. Realizing that Amma's hands were behind this, I prostrated to those people in my heart and returned home.

The flow of Amma's love enabled me to feel like I was a child before everyone. Her advice to be a beginner always eliminated all opportunities for the ego to rear its ugly head. I left only after getting precise instructions on how to go back. When I reached the temple, I felt like resting for some time under the banyan tree.

There was a small, old, dilapidated shrine behind the battered walls of the temple. I sat for some time under the banyan tree. I didn't realize that I continued sitting there until daybreak. I tried to recall what had happened. When I saw the flowers in my lap, I slowly began to recollect the events that had taken place...

When I sat under the banyan tree, it started raining. The wind caused many flowers to fall in my lap. When I tried to get up, I found that I couldn't; I couldn't even move! I felt distressed. Suddenly, the fragrance of jasmine flowers permeated the whole place. I didn't have to guess whose hands were caressing me. A presence that the moonlight didn't illumine transported me into the realm of divine bliss—one of those rare moments when time disappears. When I woke up, I began sobbing like a child. When one has imbibed the love of the universal mother, one will not get attached to anything else thereafter. Falling headlong into the pond, and later stumbling into the divine experience—I understood that everything had happened by the grace of Jagadīśvari, the Goddess of the Universe. The peace I experienced under the banyan tree was the same peace I enjoy while sitting by Amma's side. With tear-filled eyes, I recalled Amma's words: "Amma is not confined to this body."

Trials While Seeking God

8

Many did not have a proper understanding of Amma's bhāva darśans. Most were of the view that the spirit of Kṛshṇa or Devi possessed Amma during the bhāva darśans. I too had my doubts on this matter. Kṛshṇa and Devi possessing someone's body? Destroying blind faith was my goal when I first started searching for God!

I started scrutinizing Amma very closely during the bhāva darśans. Even though my intellect could not accept it, the sheer extraordinariness of what I was seeing stumped me. The spontaneity and perfection of Amma's every move won me over. What exactly was a bhāva darśan? What happens to Amma during that time?

What makes Amma divine is the fullness of her bhāvas. While in a maternal mood, she is a mother who showers affection. If she assumes the Guru Bhāva, Amma will be a strict master. While she is in Kṛshṇa Bhāva, she is the darling of Ambāḍi[14] who makes everyone laugh with her pranks. In Devi Bhāva, she is Parāśakti, the Mother of the Universe. The fullness of these bhāvas can be seen only in God. One will never perceive that plenitude in any human act, which will be trailed by the shadows of limitation and artificiality.

[14] Place where Lord Kṛshṇa grew up.

Once, while studying in school, I went for a flute recital. I was totally captivated! I badly wanted to learn how to play the flute, but my father was not in favor of it; he disapproved of anything that would take my attention away from schoolwork.

One day, I saw a man playing the flute beautifully in a nearby temple where some festivities were taking place. Near him, a few flutes were on sale. I bought one and tried to learn how to play it on my own. It was too difficult. I realized I needed a Guru who could teach me how to play the flute. I disclosed my problem to my grandmother.

She offered a suggestion. She said it would be enough if I prayed to Lord Kṛshṇa, the best flautist ever. He would certainly teach me! My grandmother guaranteed it. I trusted her. I went to a Kṛshṇa temple and prayed to the Lord to become my flute teacher. My prayers were answered—in no time at all, I was able to play a few simple songs on the flute. I was on cloud nine!

I decided to test Amma to see if she could remember how Lord Kṛshṇa had blessed me to learn the flute. Once, while Kṛshṇa Bhāva was going on, I wrapped the flute in paper and brought it to the kaḷari. Showing Amma the parcel, I asked her if she could tell me what was in it. She replied, laughing, "Son, you tell me."

I said, "I know what's in it. I was the one who wrapped it. I want to hear Amma say it."

Amma only laughed in response. Finally, she made me say it. Thinking that Amma had failed to figure out what it was, I told her it was a flute.

Then Amma said, "Son, there's no flute in there. It's a cylinder of incense sticks!"

"Amma, you've got it wrong!"

When I jubilantly declared that it was my flute and that I had wrapped it myself, Amma asked me to unwrap it. As everyone stood watching anxiously, I unwrapped the parcel. What I saw left me stunned. It was a metal cylinder containing incense sticks! I couldn't believe my eyes. How had this happened?

"Amma, are you a magician? You've changed a flute into a cylinder of incense sticks!" I did not wish to test Amma any further, but I wanted my flute back. I asked, "Where's my flute?"

"I don't know. Weren't you the one who wrapped it?"

Unable to answer her question, I stood dumbstruck. Moments later, Amma said, "It's behind the picture of Lord Kṛshṇa in the pūja room of your house."

I returned home at once and, entering the pūja room, started looking for the flute. True enough, it was exactly where Amma had said it would be. How had this happened? I was astounded! I decided to thoroughly investigate the matter. I tried to recall what had happened that day in chronological order.

That day, when I was about to leave the house after wrapping the flute, I heard my pūrvāśram mother calling from the kitchen, "Son, go only after you've had something to eat."

Since it was too early, I didn't want to eat anything. However, as my mom insisted again, I left the wrapped flute on the table in the living room and went to the kitchen to have my breakfast. That was when my father returned home, with a paper-wrapped cylinder of incense sticks. Before entering the pūja room, he went to the bathroom to wash his legs, leaving the incense stick package on the table. After washing his legs, he inadvertently picked up the wrapped flute instead of the incense sticks and put it behind the picture of Lord Kṛshṇa, where he usually kept incense sticks. When I returned from the kitchen, I picked up the parcel I saw on the table, thinking it was the flute with which I intended to test Amma, and quickly walked to the bus stop. I wasn't aware then that fun-loving Amma had already swapped the two parcels in order to pull a fast one on me. I rejoiced when I realized that I hadn't lost my flute. I also realized that admitting defeat before someone you love is a matter of great bliss.

In the *Mahābhārata*, there is an incident that occurred during the years the Paṇḍavas spent incognito. One day, Lord Kṛshṇa met the Paṇḍavas. He lay down, resting his head on Arjuna's lap, and started talking to him. He asked, "Arjuna, do you see the crow over there?"

Arjuna looked carefully and said, "Yes, my Lord, I see the crow."

The Lord then said, "I think it's a cuckoo."

Arjuna replied, "Yes, it's certainly a cuckoo."

The Lord then said, "Arjuna, it's not a cuckoo but a peachick."

Even then Arjuna said, "You're right. I can see that it's a beautiful peachick."

The Lord then said, "Arjuna, actually, it's neither a crow, cuckoo nor a peachick. It's really a vulture." He continued. "You can see with your own eyes and tell what kind of bird it is. That being the case, why did you agree with everything I said?"

Arjuna's reply was worthy of a true devotee. "O Lord, as You are omnipotent, You can change a crow into a cuckoo, a cuckoo into a peachick. I know that Your perception is more correct than mine."

With this story in mind, I put an end to my inclination to test Amma. Showering us amply with affection, Amma is striving to lead us to the windows of life's mysteries. She is creating situations that one day will rouse us from sleep and take us to those windows. We must unceasingly strive to elevate our perspective. We should develop our spiritual outlook so that we can behold God. We will then be able to sing in the intoxication of bliss, like Amma. A Guru like Amma is like a bridge that can take us to the supreme state. This bridge has two ends; one is on the shore we're on, and the other takes us to the shore of Immortality. That's why it is said that the Guru is greater than God.

Once, a mahātma said, "I can renounce God, but I can never give up my Guru. The reason is, God blessed me with this life, but the Guru liberated me from the meshes of Māyā."

That said, a Guru like Amma is both close and far away. We can feel Amma's motherly affection. At the same time, she is not attached to our material bodies and is always immersed in the ocean of supreme bliss. In that sense, you can say that she is far away. Jesus Christ said, "I am the path and the Goal." When we have developed a bond with the Guru, She will be a bridge that will take us to the supreme goal. If that is to happen, we should have intense love for the Guru. That love will lead us to the endless shores of the ocean of bliss. The Guru illumines our way with the clear light of understanding. All that the Guru does is to clarify and restore our divine vision. In that clarity, anything becomes possible.

Amma says that in order to attain the supreme goal, staunch faith is necessary. If we remain with her, we will realize that nothing is impossible. Every individual is a person of immense strength because divinity inheres in everyone. The source of our being is God, but the human mind forgets this. Imagining themselves to be devoid of such strength, people strive to gain strength through artificial means, i.e. money, power or strength. That is what millions of people are doing. However, they are looking in the wrong places. Without the ocean, the waves cannot be. A wave is nothing but a swell of the ocean. It is the natural, blissful play of the sea. The wave is possessed of superlative strength. However, it realizes this strength only when it becomes aware that it is a manifestation of the vast ocean.

The wave may forget this. Even if it doesn't even know what an ocean is, it is still in that ocean. Amma, the ocean of compassion, is here with us today to help us become aware of our real nature.

I recall an incident that happened during one of Amma's Kṛshṇa Bhāva darśans. During Kṛshṇa Bhāva, Amma would give darśan while standing with one foot placed on a pedestal. One would clearly be able to see her whole body vibrating. The clothes and ornaments that devotees adorned her with would shimmer as her body vibrated. There would be a mischievous smile on her face as she looked to the sides. Even the color of her skin would turn dark blue! Her divine beauty was ineffable. The mass of devotees would get absorbed in the fervor of devotional songs and experience heavenly bliss. Scenes of devotees who had come bearing hearts heavy with sorrow thereafter cracking up in laughter were common during Kṛshṇa Bhāva. Those who had come to tell their sorrows would often not get an opportunity to do so; their mouths would either be stuffed with cut banana pieces or they would have water from the water-pot poured continuously into their mouths! In the end, they would forget all their sorrows and leave laughing. Even though they wouldn't be allowed to say anything, I noticed that the solution to all their problems would be whispered into their ears. How does Amma know the minds of others? Would she be able to understand my mind? Or does she know only what she can see with her eyes? I tried to test her.

With her compassion-filled gaze and touch, Amma would bless the flock of devotees who stood amazed at the power she wielded, a power that can create heaven on earth. Devotees longed for an opportunity to stand near Amma and fan her. They didn't hesitate to compete for that opportunity either. That day, I got the chance to fan her. Although I fanned her for a long time, I did not get tired at all and, therefore, did not feel like passing the hand-fan to those who asked me for it. During Kṛshṇa Bhāva, Amma would, from time to time, move to the entrance of the kaḷari and gaze at the devotees waiting outside. Forgetting everything in the intoxication of the bhajans, the devotees would dance in bliss when they saw that bewitching form.

Amma moved toward the door of the kaḷari. Gazing at the swell of devotees outside, Amma stood swaying from side to side. The fervor of those singing bhajans increased. Their voices rose. Amma's *tejas* [spiritual radiance] seemed to have become concentrated on her face.

I looked near the pedestal, where Amma had placed her foot. There was a vessel there, containing the cut banana pieces that Amma would put as prasād into the mouths of the devotees. No one was watching me. All eyes were on Amma. I grabbed one of the banana pieces and stuffed it into my mouth. Amma was, even then, looking outside. I wanted to know if she knew what I had done. After 10 minutes, Amma returned to where the pedestal was. By then, I had already swallowed the banana piece. Amma looked at me and smiled. Turning to the devotees standing all around, she said, "Be careful! There's a thief here!"

Only Amma and I understood what had happened. The others did not. Amma took one of the shawls she was wearing and, using one end, tied my hands together. The other end she tied around her waist. Many hours passed. Because of the sheer size of the crowd of devotees, darśan went on for a long time. At the end of the darśan, Amma whispered into my ears, "Son, Amma noticed your prank."

"I now realize Amma has eyes even on the back of her head!" Hearing my rejoinder, Amma smiled. She untied my hands. By then, Amma had bound my soul forever to hers with cords of love that can never be untied.

The Sweetness of Death

9

Everyone fears death. The longing to preserve life is equally strong in all beings. Death is a divine experience. It often becomes our Guru. It was only when he knew he was going to die that King Parikshit became dispassionate. It was the preoccupation with death that set Prince Siddhārtha on the path to Buddhahood.

The truth is that only those who have done good deeds and led a pure life can relish death. Amma blessed me with yet another experience that taught me the greatest secrets of death.

After meeting Amma, it was usual for me to leave the college during the weekends to rush to Vaḷḷickāvu. On Monday morning, Amma herself would force me to go to college. One Monday morning, when I went to bid farewell to her, she told me not to go that day. I was overjoyed! I was thus able to spend that whole day with Amma.

She herself prepared food for me to eat. She made me sit beside her and meditate for a long time. I realized later that Amma had done all that to prepare me for a new birth.

That evening, after bhajans, while Bālagopāl (Swāmi Amṛtasvarupānanda Puri) and I were standing behind the kaḷari and talking, a snake bit me. Blood started oozing from the wound on my leg. We stood stunned, not knowing what to do. Slowly, I sat down. Suddenly, from out of the blue, Amma appeared. She started sucking the blood from the wound.

She then brought some consecrated water from the kaḷari, chanted some mantras and asked me to sip it. The pain started worsening. After some time, it became increasingly difficult for me even to sit. Amma made me lie down on her lap and she started meditating. I was aware of my hands and legs becoming numb and my breathing slowing down. As I lay in Amma's lap, I prepared myself to face death, which had come all of a sudden. Could there be a greater fortune than dying in Amma's lap?

The life-consciousness that was separating itself from the body made of the five elements was taking me to another realm. I was able to see my own inert body lying in Amma's lap. Even dying was becoming a delectable experience. That is what happens in a mahātma's presence.

Those who were present gathered around me helplessly, not knowing what to do. Some of our neighbors insisted that I should be taken to a traditional healer of snakebites. Without asking permission from Amma, who was absorbed in meditation, some carried me away to the healer. The healer, however, said that we had come too late, and that he could do nothing. In the end, they had to bring me back to Amma. She was still absorbed in meditation.

When light started to dawn, I opened my eyes. The pain in my leg had gone away completely. It was as if everything had been a dream. I wasn't in the least bit tired. The next day, I asked Amma, "Why did this happen? And that too in Amma's presence?"

She crumpled a piece of paper that was in her hand into the shape of a ball and tossed it upward. Then, catching it with her other hand, she said, "An object that is thrown up will come down. It's a law of nature. However, you can stop it from coming down with the other hand. Prayer and good deeds can mitigate the fruits of karma. One does not need to be enslaved by destiny. This would have happened no matter where you had been. Amma knows that if you're here, you won't fear. That's why Amma told you not to go to college that day."

When I went home and consulted my horoscope, I, who had no faith in astrology, was astonished. According to my horoscope, there was a strong likelihood that I would be bitten by a snake in my 21st year, thus endangering my life. It was suggested that I visit many temples, make many offerings and perform pūjas to ward off the malefic destiny.

The chart for the rest of my life had not been cast in my horoscope; it merely recorded that a future was doubtful.

That incident opened my eyes to the fact that a mahātma's sankalpa has the power to help us overcome even destiny. It also turned out to be a blessing because it helped me get permission from my family members to lead a spiritual life.

Oṇam Always

10

JUST HEARING THE word 'Oṇam'[15] will gladden the minds of anyone from Kerala. It is the one time in a year when we can forget all our sorrows. During those 10 days, we can revel in the nostalgia of a trouble-free age marked by the beauty of equality.

As a child, I had often wished that it could be Oṇam always. How happy everyone is during Oṇam! How much love and co-operation there is! The joy people felt during Oṇam greatly relieved the pain I used to feel when I saw people suffering. When I learned that there used to be a time when it was like Oṇam always, I was amazed. How had that been lost? Who was responsible for it? When I inquired into it, I found out—Lord Vishṇu Himself was the cause of it! When I saw a picture in my second-grade textbook of Vāmana standing with a foot on Mahābali's head, I was furious with Vishṇu! Wasn't it because the Lord took Mahābali away from here that all problems started? It was only years later that

[15] Kerala's harvest festival. One of the most popular festivals, it is celebrated over 10 days. It is associated with the legend of Mahābali's encounter with Vāmana. Mahābali was a kind and just ruler whose utopian rule endeared him to all his subjects. His only shortcoming was that he was too proud of his generosity. Once, while he was distributing goods to his subjects, a young Brāhmin boy, Vāmana, approached him and asked for land that could be measured by three paces. Seeing his small size, Mahābali patronizingly agreed. Vāmana, who was actually none other than Lord Vishṇu, grew. With one pace, he covered the entire earth. With the second, he covered all the other regions of the universe. Having nothing else to offer him, Mahābali offered his head for the third step. This gesture symbolizes the surrendering of the ego. Lord Vishṇu banished him to the nether world and became the guard to Mahābali's abode. It is said that on Onam, Mahābali comes to earth to see how his former subjects are doing.

I realized that we can re-create the ambience of Oṇam even in Mahābali's absence.

In the presence of Amma, the Mother of the Universe, it's always Oṇam. People forget differences of caste and creed. Foes become friends. Where else can we see the sight of rich and poor, learned and illiterate, forgetting notions of differences and coming together as Amma's darling children?

Memories of the first Oṇam after meeting Amma are still fresh in my mind.

The eve of that Oṇam—after darśan, Amma spoke to us. "Tomorrow is Oṇam. Children, you should come," she said to me and the few people who were with me.

Since it was Oṇam, my family members forbade me from going out until after I had eaten the Oṇam lunch; they were not so close to Amma then. Amma had called us so that we could eat with her. How to leave the house? By the time the cooking was over, it was already half past eleven. As soon as I had finished lunch, I left for Vaḷḷickāvu. As the buses were packed, none were stopping. I waited a long time at the bus stop. Although it came very late, the bus I boarded took me from Harippāḍ straight to Vaḷḷickāvu. It was 3:30 p.m. when I got there. I crossed the backwaters and hurried to the kaḷari. I can never forget what I saw there; it was so poignant!

Amma was lying on the bare ground, sleeping. Next to her was a stove. The earthen pot placed on it contained *chempu*[16] that crows were pecking and eating. Some pieces had fallen out of the pot and were scattered here and there.

I couldn't understand a thing. I stood still, like a statue. Slowly, I walked toward Amma and sat down next to her. The eagle that was always to be seen in the āśram was there, as if standing guard.

Later, Amma herself explained what had happened. "Hadn't Amma told her children to come? Amma was wondering what she

---

[16] Colocasia, a kind of tuber.

would give her children when they came. Amma doesn't like to ask her family members for anything. She made a stove outside, got some chempu from the vegetable patch and put them in the pot to steam them. After it had become sufficiently soft, Amma left it covered, extinguished the fire and waited for you children. Ever so often, Amma would go to the jetty to see if you had come. Amma also hasn't eaten anything. When it became very late, Amma lay on the ground and thought, 'Did I make a mistake in inviting the children. Since it's Oṇam, will their families let them go?'"

At that time, a crow pecked a steamed piece of chempu and flew away. Amma sprang up. Some pieces from the pot had fallen outside. More crows appeared to eat the pieces. "Now, what can I give my children?" Amma felt sad. She pretended to shoo the crows away. The next moment, she thought, "They too are my children. Let them eat." Amma lay on the ground again.

After a while, some of her children came. Everyone had brought Amma something. She grabbed hold of everyone and made them sit around her. She unwrapped the gifts and distributed jaggery-and-banana sweets and other confectionery to everyone. Amma smiled at everyone, her eyes brimming with tears. The sight of that innocent smile made us all cry.

Every year thereafter, we would have Oṇam lunch only with Amma. We would go to our houses, and then come to Amma by afternoon, to have our Oṇam feast!

Today, no one around Amma gives much thought to Oṇam, for every day is Oṇam! How can there be sorrow in Amma's presence? Just as snow melts in the heat of the sun, all sorrows melt away from the hearts of those who have taken refuge in Amma, the all-auspicious one.

Message of Sunrise

11

The majestic faces of the stars had started to fade. Everywhere, Nature had already started making arrangements to welcome dawn. Those nocturnal queens who had glittered regally were now disappearing.

Hearing the prayerful hymns of birds, a yogi who had been absorbed in *tapas* [austerity] opened his eyes. It was almost sunrise. There was only one star that hadn't disappeared yet. It would continue twinkling a little more, and then it too would vanish from sight. A gentle smile spread on the lips of the yogi.

The scenes of nature alert us to the impermanence of the world. We cannot depend on anything in this world. We cannot hang on to anything. Those who have realized the transience of the world strive to become free from all bondage. They thus grow more and more worthy of divine experiences until, at last, they become one with the ocean of Brahman.

People today are in a rush. How many lives have been lost in that rush! By the time we realize that nothing we sought is permanent, it's too late. All that we accumulated in the journey of life became causes of sorrow. In spite of that, expectations never cease. Only when we get everything that we yearned for do we realize that there was no gain at all. That's the only thing that remains—dissatisfaction.

Those who don't know how to strum the *vīṇa*[17] of life produce false notes of unease. In order to create a flow of everlasting music, the divine touch is necessary. The soul's music awakens the heavenly experiences of *rāga* and *tāḷa*, melody and rhythm. If we don't want the vīṇa of our life to become useless, we should first learn how to use it. We can never figure out intellectually where the music in the vīṇa is, but the musician's heart and fingers know! The heart can fathom the truth that the intellect cannot unearth. It's a divine experience to which only the pure heart can lay claim.

Amma used to say, "Children, every moment is precious. Even losing one crore rupees isn't so bad, but you shouldn't lose even a second. We can always regain the wealth we lose, but we can never recover the time we waste."

Once, a *brahmacāri* was sent to Kāyāmkuḷam to buy some necessities for the āśram. Unable to get a bus even after waiting for a long time, he returned by taxi. He told Amma what he had done. She asked, "Son, why did you spend money unnecessarily? Even though you would have been late, couldn't you have come back by bus?"

With all humility, the brahmacāri replied, "Amma, didn't you say it's better to lose one crore rupees than to lose even a second? It was only after wasting an hour of my time waiting for the bus that I decided to take a taxi."

---

[17] A traditional Indian stringed instrument.

Amma replied, "Who said it would be wasting time? Couldn't you have chanted your mantra or cleaned the bus stop while waiting? Allowing your mind to wander is the biggest crime. The mind that's habituated to roaming around is what takes us away from God. Never give the mind an opportunity to be idle."

During the early days with Amma, I once heard some householder devotees complain to Amma, "Amma, why do you show so much love to these college students?" They had become upset seeing her shower us with the loving affection that mothers shower on their young ones. Everyone wants Amma's love. All beings, moving and unmoving, crave her caresses. I have seen even birds and beasts competing for Amma's affection, never mind human beings! A knower of Truth becomes the center of attraction for everyone. We inadvertently wish, *If only Amma looked this way, If only Amma smiled at me, If only she uttered a word to me, If only she would come near me...* Amma is in the process of binding us all by the cord of Love.

"Not even one of these college students may be good"—they tried to remind Amma yet again. As soon as they started complaining, Amma's expressions of love intensified. We were thus able to see how the complaints and taunts of others could turn into blessings. "Amma, why do you spend so much time with them?" Hearing this, she smiled.

Unable to understand the meaning of her smile, they asked, "Amma, why are you smiling?"

"What else can I do but smile? Suppose someone asks, 'Doctor, why do you waste your time seeing the sick who come to the hospital? Isn't it enough to see just the healthy?' can the doctor help not smiling? The hospital is for the sick. The healthy don't need to be healed." Finally, to reassure the complainants, Amma said, "Children, don't be upset. If I have spent time with them, I will extract the price with interest."

When they heard it, they felt consoled. They came and told us, “Amma said she would extract the price with interest.”

“What interest?” I asked incredulously. Amma had said that she would demand interest on the time she had spent with us. Hearing the word ‘interest,’ I inadvertently started laughing. It was only when I reflected on Amma’s words later that I began to realize their significance.

If I have spent time with them, I will extract the price with interest—Even the complainants wouldn’t have imagined how high the interest would be; that we would have to pledge our very lives. This is the way of the Guru. The disciple understands the truth that nothing he offers the Guru can measure up to Her love and sacrifice. The disciple surrenders to the Guru in the same way that a proprietor, unable to repay a loan, permits the bank to confiscate his property. However, the disciple surrenders, not crying like the proprietor, but shedding tears of joy. He realizes that nothing acquired was really a gain, and that there is no one else to rely on. Realizing his helplessness, the disciple seeks refuge at the feet of the Guru. He surrenders his very life to the Guru, and thus enjoys the bliss of self-surrender.

An example of the ideal Guru is Vāmana, who covered the worlds ruled over by King Mahābali with just two steps. The Guru takes on all the *prārabdha* [karmic burden] of the disciple who makes an offering of the ego. The story of Mahābali who sacrificed himself has become immortal. The ego is indeed the greatest sacrifice one can make to the Lord, and this is what Mahābali did.

The union of Guru and disciple is that singular moment when one merges with unbroken consciousness, during which one experiences the sacred ecstasy arising from the indescribable, priceless moments of self-surrender. After one has surrendered one’s individuality, life in this world becomes unnecessary; one dwells in the Guru’s world. There, the Guru is the Guard. Lord Vishṇu is Mahābali’s protector. This security is more worthy of our faith than any other kind of security arrangement. This is what the presence of the Guru is like. Can there be anything more precious than getting the Lord as one's protector? That's what Mahābali got. The Guru places Her feet on the head of the noblest disciple who is ready to surrender his whole life at the Guru's holy feet. By trampling upon the ego, the Guru awakens Self-awareness.

The Guru is like the gardener who perceives the huge tree in the seed. No seed is considered infertile. The gardener can see the flowers that are going to blossom on that tree and the fruits that are going to emerge from those flowers. Similarly, as far as the Guru is concerned, no object is useless. She sees only the pulsations of unbroken consciousness everywhere. The sculptor doesn't see the stone, only the sculpted form of divinity. The Guru takes on the karmic burden of the disciple who surrenders herself. She guides such a disciple to eternal freedom.

The Guru is one who sees the infinite potentialities within us. She takes us from blind faith to Self-confidence, or faith in the Self. The Guru bestows upon the disciple the wings of devotion and faith with which he can fly from the bondage to perishable objects to the endless skies of the Imperishable. When one has been relieved of the ego's burden, one can soar effortlessly into the empyrean heights. In order to make the flight into the world of the Self effortless, we must surrender ourselves to the Lord.

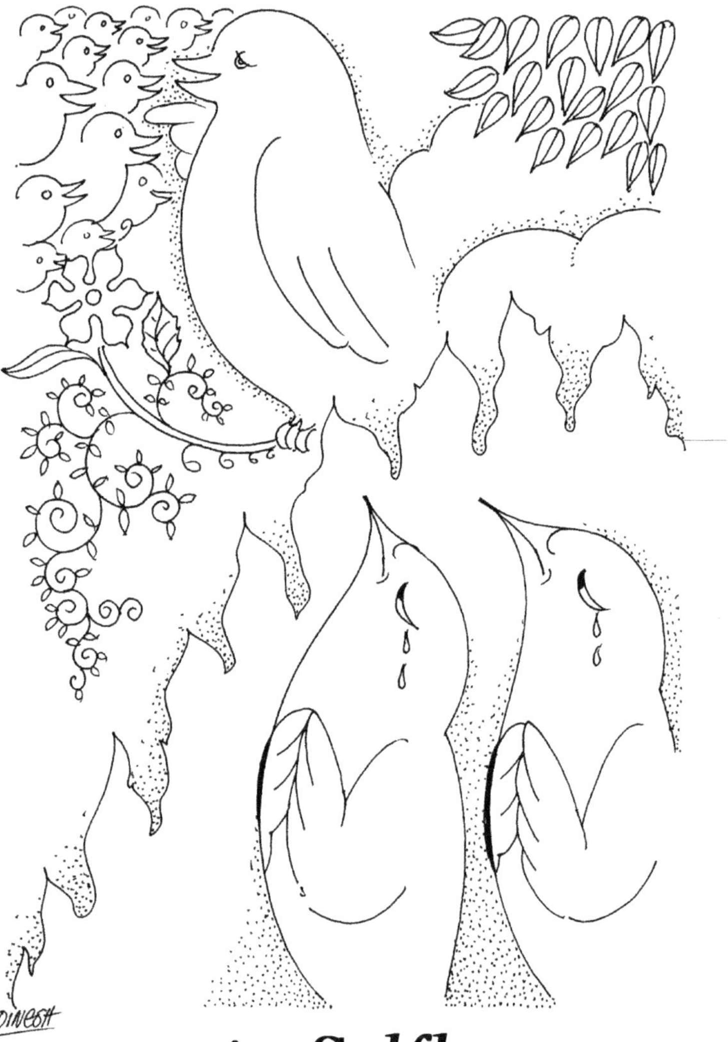

Lessons in Selflessness

12

THE EXPERIENCES I had after meeting Amma turned my life around completely. By thinking about Amma all the time, I was able to forget other things easily, even though that forgetfulness created other problems. Nevertheless, the bliss it conferred was boundless. In any case, don't we meditate, chant our mantras and do pūja in order to forget everything else? It's when we forget everything else that God dawns within our hearts; or, we forget everything in His presence. This is what happened to me also.

"Is it right for an educated youth like you to give in to blind faith?"

I could smile before the doubts and taunts of my friends. How could experience be blind faith? I didn't bother to explain. The fact was, the divine intoxication Amma had infused in me had removed even the zeal for arguing.

College closed for the mid-summer holidays, making it possible for us to visit Amma daily. On most days, Bālagopāl and I would visit Amma together. Amma's father didn't like outsiders spending too much time there. There was no āśram then; it was only Amma's house. Nonetheless, we were able to spend the whole day with Amma. The nights we would spend in the open ground near the Occira temple, meditating at the grove there. The closer we got to Amma, the more obstacles it seemed we had to face.

In those days, Amma had more householder children than monastic disciples. Everyone wanted Amma to show him or her special affection and love. This led to stiff competition among the householder devotees. Some of them didn't like the fact that Bālagopāl and I were coming to the āśram increasingly often and staying there. We were always together. We would come for darśan together, sing bhajans together, and meditate together. Because of this, Amma used to call us twins. On the days we visited Amma, she would spend more time with us than with others. We weren't aware that this was breeding resentment among some of the householder devotees. They began to harbor grudges against us, thinking that Amma loved us more, and that she wasn't giving them any attention.

One day, the householder devotees came together and complained to Amma. "After these college students started coming, we haven't been able to enjoy Little One's undivided attention." In those days, devotees would address Amma as "Little One," "Amma" or as "Little Ammachi." Sometimes, she would behave like a child. At other times, she would be in the bhāva of a Mother or of Devi. Everyone interpreted the līlās of the Universal Mother's incarnation in their own ways. "They're not here because of devotion, but to get Little One's love," they said. They didn't even hesitate to tell Amma not to give undue importance to us, as we were only pretending to have devotion.

From the next day onward, Amma stopped talking to us altogether. She didn't even look at us. Even when we prostrated before her, Amma would look in some other direction. Or she would sit with eyes closed. If not that, she would tell someone else to come near her and start speaking to that person. Many days passed this way. The householder children were delighted. Amma stopped paying attention to us even during the bhāva darśans. She did not speak, smile or look at us. We became very upset, not knowing what the problem was. Previously, when we visited Amma, we would often not have eaten. Amma herself would come to us and insist that we eat, but now there was no one to insist. Because of that, we were starving. Amma's cold-shoulder treatment broke our spirits. We felt as if we were losing our minds! We forgot to eat and sleep. Many days passed. We sat alone and cried without anyone noticing us. Nevertheless, we were unable to stay away from Amma. We continued going to see her.

One day, when we reached the āśram, Amma was in the coconut grove in front of the kaḷari. She was surrounded on all sides by householder devotees. Everyone was roaring with laughter, seeing Amma's antics. We stood at a distance, as still as statues, watching the scene. Slowly, we walked toward her, prostrated, and then entered the kaḷari, closing the door behind us. Amma's love saturated even the tears flowing down our cheeks.

Suddenly, Amma opened the door and came inside. She embraced us with both arms. Her eyes were filled with tears. No one was able to speak. In those moments, I realized how much more powerful than words silence is. After a long time, Amma broke the silence.

"Children, do you have any grudge against Amma? It's not because Amma likes to hurt her children. She had to do this to show the others the surrender you children have. When your hearts ached, Amma's heart broke. Some people are under the impression that it was only because Amma is showing you love that you're coming here. They claim that it's not because of devotion or faith. Amma had no other way to prove your innocence to these people. Amma knows that no matter how cruelly she behaves, you will continue to come here, whereas if I don't speak to them for just one day, many of them will stop coming later." Amma said all this within earshot of the others. She had to act like a child before those who called her "Little One." I realized then that any bhāva Amma adopts is only for our good. She yet again strengthened our conviction that we are ever safe in her hands. Before long, many of the jealous householder children had to part company with Amma.

Amma used to say, "Children, those who have no mental purity cannot remain here for too long. This soil has been soaked by Amma's teardrops. Even the grains of sand here are charged with the power of mantras. This place is a center of selflessness. This soil is for innocent hearts. It is a sanctuary for the grieving. It's not a place for nurturing one's ego. Anyone who stands in the way of those striving to sustain its purity will have to leave this place."

We became aware in hindsight that Amma's words had been literally true. We should forget our selfishness and unite as children of one Mother, at least in the presence of mahātmas. Gradually, we must realize the truth that Amma's family has expanded to include the whole world. When we develop the heart to see the whole world as our own and love it thus, the river of Amma's grace will take us to the ocean of *sat-cit-ānanda*, knowledge-existence-bliss.

VIMAL

An Atheist's Change of Heart

13

All around us, we can see people deriding the great Gurus, mocking them with the label 'human gods.' Those who know that everything is divine do not see the human; they behold only God everywhere. For those who have perceived divine energy palpitating in moving and unmoving creatures, in the biggest and smallest, in trees and in a poisonous snake, the cosmos itself is God. In that awareness, the dewdrop and the great ocean vanish. The knower, the known and the knowing all dissolve in the ocean of Brahman. The wise who have realized that they are the witness consciousness abiding in all things do not regard themselves as the body; other people think they have bodies. Devotees thought that Lord Kṛshṇa had incarnated. However, the Lord knew, even when He was enacting the līlās through the dark-blue-hued body, that He was all-pervasive. The limitations of the body do not constrain the omnipresence of mahātmas. Ordinary people cannot even imagine the experiences of knowers of Truth. In spite of that, human beings make the futile attempt of trying to measure the jñānis with the limited yardstick of their own puny intellects. God, who is of the nature of one's own Self, can never be realized through the vanity of scholarship.

Once, I met some of my relatives from North Kerala in my pūrvāśram. One of them was a staunch atheist and an admirer of Karl Marx. He spoke at length about communism and rational thinking. When he started criticizing Amma, I objected, but, unable to express my experience in words, began floundering. I had only started learning the ABCs of spirituality. No matter how much I tried to tell him about the intoxication of divine love and its ability to revolutionize one's outlook on life, he remained unconvinced. He too started belittling my words, using that derisive term 'human gods.'

I didn't feel any satisfaction either, no matter how much I tried to talk about Amma. Finally, I started praying to Amma herself. "O Mother, I am incapable of extolling your infinite glories. Please deign to make this man realize your greatness." Later, when I went to see Amma, I reminded her about this matter. I didn't even hesitate to tell her that she should punish him. Hearing this, Amma laughed for a long time.

She then said, "Son, one must have done good deeds in past lives to be deserving of being punished by God. Amma has no intention of punishing those who don't believe in her or those who ridicule her. Amma is striving to make them do good deeds and thus transform them into blessed souls." Her words shed light on the purpose of her incarnation.

I forgot about that incident. Many months passed before I ran into that atheist again. I was amazed. He was a completely changed man. There was a sandal-paste mark on his forehead. He was wearing white clothes and there was an amulet tied around his wrist.

"What's all this about? What happened?" I asked in utter amazement.

"Oh, nothing," he said evasively with a wan smile.

I pressed him to speak. When he saw that I did not intend to let him off, he was ready to open up. He told me about an incident that happened months before, after he had criticized Amma.

It must have been after one o'clock at night. He was walking home quickly after a long trip. Since he had missed the night bus from town, he decided to take a short cut through a field. That route was fraught with dangers, but since he was familiar with it, having taken that path many times before, it wasn't too difficult for him to get home. It was pitch dark all around. In the dim light of his torch, he couldn't see the path clearly at all; the moonlight did a better job than his torchlight in illumining the path before him. He had to cross a brook running alongside the path he was taking. The place was known to be infested with poisonous snakes. When he stepped into the waters, he felt as if someone was following him. He turned around and saw the form of a woman clad in pure-white clothes. In that total darkness, only her face was indistinct. When he directed the torch light in that direction, he didn't see anyone. He thought that the soft moonlight must have conjured an illusion in the darkness; thus reassuring himself, he walked on. When he heard the sound of footsteps behind him, he turned around again. It was that same form, yet again. Shining his torch, he walked toward the place where he had seen the form. The form of the woman then reappeared elsewhere. He walked toward *that* spot. Whenever he walked toward the form, it would move to another spot. He thus spent a lot of time walking around the place. He didn't feel frightened in the least. By the time he got home, everyone had already gone to sleep. Only his room, which was on the upper floor, was unlocked. Someone had placed in that room the account book from the office of the political party he was a member of. He sat down in a chair, thinking that he would look through the book before turning in.

"That's when it happened!"

I noticed that his facial expression had changed. Fear had turned his face scarlet. His hands were trembling.

"That's when *what* happened?" I asked impatiently.

He continued the narration. Hearing a loud scream, everyone in the house woke up, even the neighbors. Everyone ran to the spot from where the scream had issued. The man lay there, unconscious. The leather-bound account book he had in his hands lay crushed like *pappaḍam*. Some people picked up the man, lying on the floor like a corpse, and laid him on the bed. They used a spoon to pry apart his jaws, and poured water into his mouth. After some time, the man opened his eyes. Slowly, he sat up in bed. Gathering up his courage, he said, "I got frightened by a nightmare."

After some time, everyone left. Hearing a scream again, they ran back. When he regained consciousness, the man explained what had happened. While examining the account book, he had been jolted by a sound. When he looked up, he saw the form he had seen in the field! He screamed and fainted. After coming to, he had again seen the form, this time more clearly. He couldn't recall what had happened after that.

That day, he was frightened various times this way. He couldn't get away. Even after many days, things didn't change. He became frightened of closing his eyes even during the day. He passed many days without sleeping. Left with no other choice, he consulted many priests. None could solve his problem. Finally, he met a priest who happened to be a devotee of Devi. That man at once realized what the problem was. The priest said, "It's nothing but the presence of Devi Herself. Don't waste your money on anything else. There is only one solution: conduct prayers to appease Devi." The man then carried out a special worship in a Devi temple for 41 days. He then began to feel some relief. After that, the priest tied an amulet around his wrist. Whenever he removed the amulet, though, the situation would revert and create problems for him.

When I heard the man's story, I couldn't help laughing. Right then, I resolved to take him to Amma. This time, he didn't object. As we were crossing the Vaḷḷickāvu backwaters, the strains of the bhajans being sung in front of the kaḷari reached our ears.

When that man saw Amma, who was sitting on the veranda of the kaḷari, absorbed in the bliss of the bhajans, he started.

"What's the matter? Why are you getting scared?" I asked.

He replied, his lips trembling, "This is the very form I used to see!"

He rushed toward Amma and fell at her feet. He broke down and cried, begging for forgiveness. Amma placed the man's head on her lap and started caressing him. She untied the consecrated amulet from his wrist.

"Son, you don't need to wear this anymore. You don't need to fear anything anymore. You need to fear only the ego within yourself. One can overcome fear with an attitude of devotion. Destroying the faith of another is equal to murdering a Brāhmin. Therefore, son, you should perform expiatory rites to confer peace on others. Those who can love others as themselves don't need temples or other places of worship. God Himself will be ready to serve such people.

"However, most are unable to work selflessly. They can't serve society more than they love their own families. Only mahātmas have been able to serve the whole world without accepting any remuneration, seeing God in everything. Real service is only possible when one has equal vision. It is from āśrams, temples and other places of worship that we get practice in seeing everyone as God. Faith in and worship of God, which will make the human mind expansive, are vital for ordinary people." Amma's words transformed that man into an ideal devotee and social worker.

It is natural for the Lord to feel compassionate toward His devotees, but I've been stunned to see Amma express that same compassion toward those we consider cruel. It's easy to love those who love us, but it's not easy to love those who insult us. Amma's abiding nature, however, is to shower love equally on those who love and those who hate.

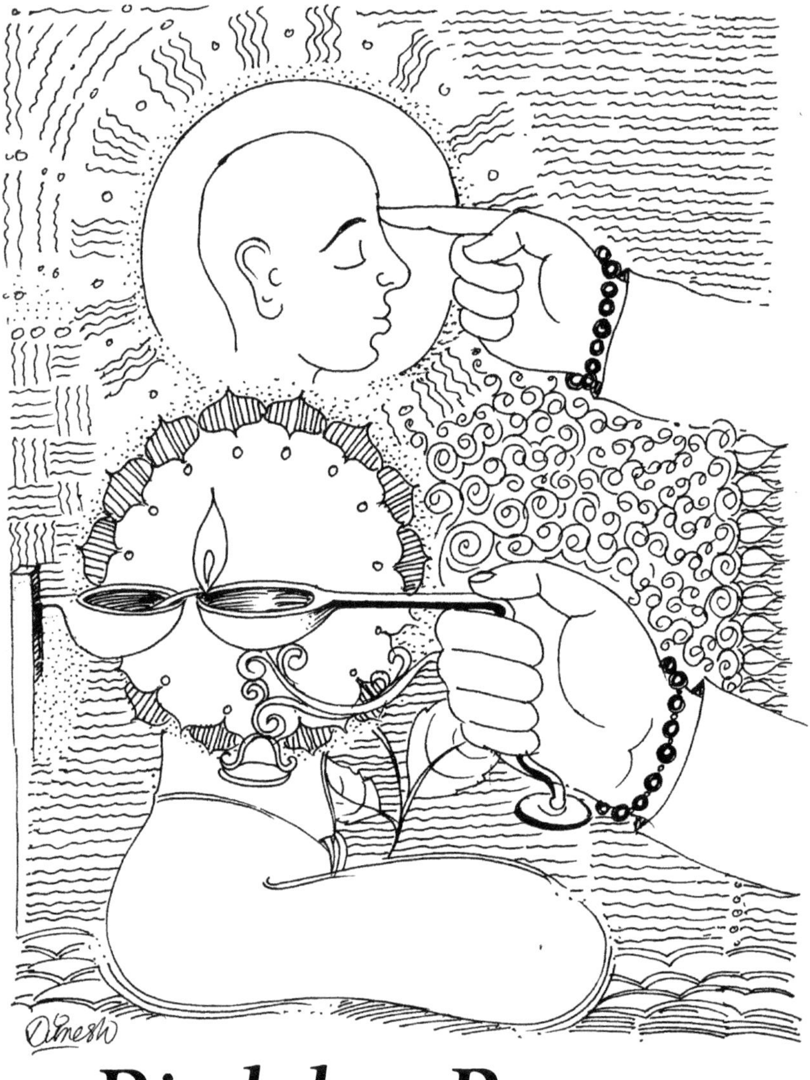

Birthday Present

14

Few dislike celebrating their birthdays. We forget the truth that every birthday we celebrate is taking us closer to death. Every birthday reminds us of the fact that our lifespan has been shortened yet again by one year. If we're born, we must die; there's no other way, is there? Anything that is born will die too. What then is the way to avoid death? Avoid birth. In other words, the idea that we were born must die. For one who knows that he is not the body but the soul, there is no death. The changes to the body do not affect him. The awareness that one is the Self that transcends the body, mind and intellect can only arise through the grace of a Satguru like Amma.

I am reminded of one of my birthdays, before I became an āśram resident. That day, I went to Vaḷḷickāvu to see Amma. It was with a mindset that attributed too much importance to birthdays that I reached there. I had in my hands the *pāyasam* [sweet pudding] I had received after performing a pūja in a temple. I hadn't eaten anything. I had gone to Vaḷḷickāvu, determined to have only what Amma offered. What birthday present would she give me?

When I reached the grounds before the kaḷari, I saw something hilarious—Amma was wrestling with Acchamma; that's what everyone called Amma's late paternal grandmother. Acchamma loved Amma's pranks. Amma saw me, but I felt she was ignoring me. This was not usually the case. She would usually run to me as soon as she saw me, but now, she was pretending not to have seen me and continuing to chat with others. Hours passed. It was twilight. Sitting in front of the kaḷari, Amma started singing bhajans.

I sat some distance away, on the open veranda of the thatched hut, and meditated. When the bhajans were about to end, Rāmakṛshṇa (now Swāmi Rāmakṛshṇānanda Puri) arrived. He was then working in Harippāḍ Bank. As soon as the bhajans were over, Amma walked past me to where Rāmakṛshṇa was seated. She did not even glance at me. Like Lord Kṛshṇa who, pretending not to have seen Duryodhana even though he had come first, started talking to Arjuna instead, Amma also spent a long time with Rāmakṛshṇa. I became angry and upset. I entered the kaḷari and closed the doors behind me.

After two hours, Amma opened the doors and came inside. I acted as if I hadn't seen her. With great compassion, Amma approached me. I didn't say anything. "Amma wanted to see just how much patience son has. Do you feel bad?"

Laughing, Amma tried to console me. She grabbed me forcefully and dragged me into the kitchen. She noticed the pāyasam I had brought with me. "Did you bring this, son?"

I did not respond to her question.

Amma ladled rice and curries into a plate. She mixed them and rolled them into balls. At first, I thought I wouldn't accept one, but when I looked at Amma's face, which was radiating so much compassion, I did not have the heart to refuse.

"Son, what's so special about today?"

I knew that it was with full knowledge of everything that she had asked the question. I said, "Today is my birthday. I've heard that a child's birthday is very important to its mother."

"Son, you were Amma's son even before you were born! How then can Amma consider this day to be your birthday? Amma doesn't feel there is anything special about it. Amma is not the mother of just the body. She is also the mother of the Self. Since the Self is never born and never dies, what birthday is there to talk about? Whose birthday?"

In the flow of Amma's wisdom, all the questions in my mind dissolved. I went to sit inside the kaḷari. Amma applied some sandal paste on my forehead. After pressing the spot between my eyebrows with her index finger for some time, Amma left the kaḷari. However, I was unable to move from that spot. What I experienced then was as amazing as death. It seemed as if I had totally lost control over my body. I could not even make a sound. Amma's shower of compassion flowed into me like a Ganges of nectar. I lost all bodily consciousness. I don't know how long I remained on those shores of Peace, utterly content.

Who could have given a better birthday present?

That inexpressible divine experience, which only the compassion of a Satguru can bestow, was a priceless gift and an ever-present reminder of Amma's glory, one that has remained luminous in the corridors of my memory.

A Sentry's Demise

15

It was a bhāva darśan day. Devotees held their breath as they watched Amma licking away the pus oozing from the wounds of a leper. I was standing in a corner of the kaḷari, watching the scene intently, without taking my eyes away. I wondered if Amma wasn't being carried away by her show of compassion. In any case, the scene didn't strike me as being too moving. When darśan ended, I told Amma that.

"Amma, being omnipotent, you can cure this disease by your mere sankalpa. Then why this particular expression?"

Amma smiled and posed another question in response. "Couldn't Lord Kṛshṇa have brought the Kauravas around through a sankalpa? Why did he become Arjuna's charioteer?" [18]

I had no answer. Even so, Amma realized that I wasn't satisfied by her answer. She continued, "Son, I don't know why. When I

[18] An allusion to the Mahābhārata war between the unrighteous Kauravas and the righteous Pāṇḍavas. When both sides approached the Lord for help, Kṛshṇa said that He would not fight in the war, but that one side could have His army, and the other side could have Him as a charioteer. Arjuna, one of the Pāṇḍavas, opted to have the Lord as his charioteer; the Kauravas chose the Lord's army.

look at that son who is afflicted with leprosy, I feel like acting this way. You will understand the reason for it in due course."

Later, I read in many books that the saliva of an enlightened soul has healing properties and that it is an infallible remedy for incurable diseases. Even then, my skepticism did not go away. What was the difference between Amma's body and that of an ordinary person? Aren't both made from *pancabhūtas?*[19] If so, what was so special about the body of an enlightened soul like Amma? I didn't broach this subject with Amma again.

Days passed. Amma was sitting in the āśram grounds, dotted with coconut trees that swayed in the breeze. Her children who tailed her like shadows were sitting around her on all sides. The āśram then was nothing more than a few huts scattered around the coconut grove, the kaḷari and the house in which Amma grew up. She rarely ate. If devotees brought any food, she would divide it among the children around her. Amma would then say, "If my children's stomachs get filled, Amma feels full."

One day, Amma opened a food packet that someone had brought and started feeding her children with balls of rice. Suddenly, there was a commotion outside. People were chasing a rabid dog. It had already bitten many people. It was one of the two dogs that had stood by Amma, like warrior guards, during her early days.

"Son!"

Amma was calling the dog. It ran toward her. "Hey, what happened to you?"

She patted it with a lot of affection. It wagged its tail, as if nothing had happened, and started burrowing its face in Amma's lap. The saliva and other things oozing from its mouth soiled her body and clothes. Amma drew the dog close to her, hugged it and kissed it on its head. She rolled the rice into balls and put them into its mouth. Then, with the same hand that was coated with the

[19] The five [panca] elements [bhutas] that are the material cause of creation.

dog's saliva, Amma started eating the rice herself. Those watching the scene were aghast. "Amma, what are you doing?" cried some of the devotees.

Amma took no heed of them. She cuddled the dog for a long time. It curled up in Amma's lap, like a small child.

"Śri-*mon*[20], go get a chain."

When I heard Amma saying this, I ran to the next house. I found a chain there and returned with it.

Amma said, "Chain the dog to the tree. Its time has come."

Did Amma really mean that the rabid dog must be tied up? I wanted to ask, "Must *I* do it?" But I held my tongue. There was no point protesting anyway. Wasn't it Amma who was telling me to do it? Reassuring myself that she would take care of me, I walked slowly with the chain toward the dog, looped the chain around its neck and dragged it to the coconut tree in front of the kaḷari. It followed me, meek as a lamb. Its demeanor seemed to indicate an awareness of its impending end. After I tied it to the tree, it breathed its last, in full view of all the onlookers. I noticed tear drops spilling from Amma's eyes.

Amma's mother, father and siblings, all of whom had learned that Amma had touched the rabid dog and eaten food with hands coated with its saliva, began wailing. There was no doubt that Amma had ingested the dog's saliva. Not only that, she had also caressed parts of the dog's body that had been wounded by stones hurled at it. For these reasons, everyone began insisting that Amma should get a rabies shot. Many of those who tried persuading Amma begged her tearfully, but Amma refused. Smiling at me, she said, "Son, shouldn't we find out if this body is made up of the pancabhūtas?"

I hung my head and, with joined palms, reined in my thoughts as I reflected upon Amma's glories. Through such experiences,

---

[20] The author's pre-monastic name was Śrikumār.

Amma taught us hidden truths that the intellect cannot grasp. The Guru imparts secrets that cannot be taught. The disciple absorbs lessons that cannot be learned. The Guru doesn't have the attitude of a teacher. The disciple doesn't realize he is learning. The divine experiences that turn on its head all the information that has been amassed will make the disciple bow down his head. Any disciple would become humble, seeing the Guru's sublime powers.

When we have attained inner purity, outer impurities will not affect us. Even if we wear unsightly clothes, there will be an overflowing beauty nonetheless. The bodies of yogis who haven't bathed or eaten for years will exude a sweet smell, owing to meditative absorption. When all the nerves are purified, the body will be free of impurities. The mere presence of such a being will purify the atmosphere. One can observe the workings of the body, considered a composite of the pancabhūtas, changing in accordance with one's inner purity. In order to acquire the natural purity of souls like Amma, we must start with external purity.

The ṛshis who were embodiments of peace remained steeped in meditation even amid wild beasts. In the presence of these ṛshis who had transcended their sense of individuality, the wild animals forgot their instinctive hostility toward human beings. The presence of mahātmas who have attained inner purity will be reflected even in nature.

The vibrations of Amma's pure love are spreading in all directions, drawing humanity together. The drops of individuality are being transformed into a mighty ocean of love and wisdom.

-VIMAL-

A Melody's Drone

16

My engineering degree examinations ended. God's testing began. On most days, I stayed in Vaḷḷickāvu. By then, all my pūrvāśram family members had become devotees of Amma, and therefore, I did not face any opposition. Nevertheless, my parents were anxious about losing their only son. Without my knowledge, my father procured a good job for me at the Rāman Research Institute in Bangalore. Even though I was adamant that I would not go there, Amma insisted that I should go and work for some time at least. No one was prepared to take my side. Amma and all the devotees who used to visit the āśram came to send me off at the railway station. I stood looking through the windows until everyone disappeared from sight.

I had to endure this separation at a time when I could not bear to be parted from Amma for even a second. Although this separation caused immense anguish, I realized later that it was nature's way of letting me behold Amma's wondrous līlās. Outside, the scenes kept changing. I mentally lauded the moving train for disregarding the changing sights. How can it run if it becomes despondent, remembering the bygone scenes? I felt as if Amma was telling me that this was just as true for the journey of life as well.

Is there anything here one can truly own? What is the point of trying to possess anything that will eventually turn to dust? This is why one takes refuge in the imperishable truth embodied by Amma. Because mahātmas are not bodily creatures, depending on them will not make our lives a fruitless enterprise. *Why continue frittering away our lives in the material world through worthless pursuits?* My mind kept repeating this question to itself. I noticed the sounds of the train becoming a lullaby. It was trying, as if with Amma's compassion, to rock me to sleep. "O Lord! I can see that You are not invisible. Have You infused even this locomotive with Amma's love?" I didn't notice when its consoling touch and crooning sounds lulled me into deep sleep.

"Aren't you getting down?" asked a railway official, shaking me awake.

I woke up with a start. Another man came near me and introduced himself. "My name is Daniel. I have been waiting for you at the station. A senior scientist asked me to escort you from the railway station. I noticed everyone alighting and began to worry when I didn't see you. I then started looking for you in every compartment. That's when I found you here. I had been given a photo to identify you."

When I pondered over how the Institute had acquired a photo of me, I was amazed. I had sent neither an application nor a photo. I didn't probe the issue any further.

Daniel took my bag and got off the train. I followed. I didn't feeling like speaking to anyone. Daniel didn't understand the reason for my reticence. "Aren't you pleased at having landed this job?"

Indeed, many dream of getting a job in the Rāman Research Institute. Without waiting to hear my response, Daniel continued talking.

I began to feel that my conduct was unbecoming. We soon reached his place of residence. I apologized to Daniel for not having said anything so far. I tried to make him understand that I had been silent owing to the mental anguish I was experiencing as a result of leaving home. Daniel was a very loving person. He quickly prepared food and, like a mother, sat next to me, coaxing me into eating something. I clearly felt that Amma was working through Daniel.

The next day, I got ready to go to the Institute. I took out a photo that I had kept safely in my bag. It was the first photo of Amma I had received—a rare photo of Amma from the old days! It was the only thing I considered an acquisition in my life so far! However, I couldn't bear to look at the photo for too long. I silently sought Amma's permission and blessings before starting out for work. I then wrapped the photo in a silk cloth and put it back in the bag. That day, I went to work at the Institute.

It was a job I had dreamed about while in school. I was assigned to the department of research on solar radiation. Before starting work, I meditated on the Sun-god, who is a symbol of wisdom. I didn't feel honored by the position that my 17 long years of education had helped me clinch. I sat in an air-conditioned room amid computers and other machines, feeling ill at ease.

The senior scientist took a great liking to me. I felt astonished when I heard everyone calling her "Amma." Unmarried, she had dedicated most of her life to research. Everyone must have started calling her "Amma," seeing her life, which was truly a testament to renunciation. I strove to console myself with the thought that I had found an environment conducive for remembering my Amma, my Satguru. Even though others referred to this scientist as "the woman who had forgotten to live," one could sense the beauty of contentment in her words when she spoke about her contributions to the scientific world. I couldn't help thinking how much more she would have accomplished if only she had endeavored to do research in the inner world.

I recalled Amma's words: "Anything is possible for one who is ready to renounce."

Even though people called her "Amma," everyone was scared of her. She was an exacting boss whom everyone tried to please by doing his or her job as sincerely and perfectly as possible. Many people here loved me. I realized that Jagadīśvari Herself was seeing to it that Her son wanted for nothing in this place. Yet, I felt no interest whatsoever in working here. I didn't want anyone's love either. I passed many a dispassionate day here, alone and in silence.

Amma made her presence felt through innumerable experiences that she bestowed every day. Later, I learned from Amma herself that those experiences were meant to show me that she is not limited to the body and that she was with me all the time. She thought that those experiences would lessen my anguish.

But they intensified my sorrow. I spent many days crying in that metropolis, bewailing my lot. I felt I was wasting my life in the midst of materialism, like a fool casting away priceless pearls for glass beads.

It had been several weeks since I left Amma and reached Bangalore. In the meantime, I had received many letters of consolation from her. I did not even have the strength to finish reading her words, which were overflowing with love. The last words I had spoken to Amma upon bidding her farewell came to mind: "Amma, bless me so that I may return soon!" Many were the days I thought of returning. On those days, Amma would appear in my dream and forbid me from doing so.

One day, when I could no longer bear the pain of separation, I disclosed everything to Daniel. His face became wan when he learned about my decision to leave. For a long time, he didn't say anything. He had already understood a great deal about me earlier. He took me to a solitary place, probably thinking that I would gain some consolation from it. It was a desolate area where mountains rose to the skies and rocks littered the ground. It had an understated rural beauty that was totally devoid of the artificiality of cities. At a distance, clouds huddled together to mourn the setting sun. There was no way the Goddess of Nature, who had witnessed untold risings and settings, would see anything new in this. How many more funerals like this were yet to take place! To whom could the pining clouds, lacking the fortitude to witness all these, pour out their woe? Before long, their enchanting forms too would disappear. The nocturnal dance of destruction would begin. Terror would have its play and, in one fell stroke, plunge those bewildered by day's myriad hues into sorrow.

But I realized the lack of clarity caused by the darkness of ignorance was far more terrifying than this night. Daniel and I slowly climbed up the mountain. The gentle breeze that had come to caress the twilight gave us some relief. We sat on a boulder and talked about Amma for a long time, gazing into the distance. Daniel then lay down on the rock. I moved a short distance away and closed my eyes, trying to meditate. An unusual thought passed through my mind—isn't it this body that is the cause of my separation from Amma? Destroy it then! Without further ado, I got up from where I was seated. I realized that Daniel was sleeping. Slowly, I moved to the other side of the boulder.

The mountains were awash in the glow of the full moon. Down below was a gaping chasm. I closed my eyes for a moment and prayed. My legs ran forward swiftly... someone yanked me with great force. I fell back. Who had pulled me? Daniel? I turned around. There was no one behind! Daniel was still lying down in the same place, sleeping. I tried to get up again, but found that I couldn't. Stunned, I remained in that position, not knowing what had happened. I felt as if my head was spinning. I remained supine on the boulder and closed my eyes, meditating on Amma. After some time, I heard her voice resounding in my ears.

"Son, committing suicide is cowardly. The body is very precious. It is a gift from God, a medium for realizing the Ātma. It is meant to give peace to many people. Destroying it is the greatest crime you can commit against the world and Amma. Rise above circumstances. Be brave! Son, move ahead without flagging. Amma is with you."

It was my Amma's voice, the voice of my inner self. Overcome by remorse, I broke down in tears. Why should I grieve, when Amma is sitting in my very heart as the antaryāmi, witnessing my every thought and deed? Laying on the rock, I looked up at the sky. The full moon was beaming. Would one ever be deprived of at least the consolation of moonlight in darkness? I looked intently at the face of the moon. There, I saw the Goddess of the Universe cuddling me with her thousand hands. From the depth of my heart, a few lines issued through my lips as poetry:

arikil undenkilum ariyān kazhiyāte
alayunnu ñān amme...
kaṇṇuṇḍennālum kāṇān kazhiyāte
tirayunnu ñān ninne... amme
tirayunnu ñān ninne

O Amma, even though you are near, I am wandering about. Even though I have eyes, I am searching, unable to see you.

hemanta nīlaniśīthiniyil pūtta
vārtingaḷ nīyāṇo...?
vānilettīḍuvān kazhiyāte tīrattil
tala tallum tiramāla ñān... amme
tala tallum tiramāla ñān

Are you the beautiful moon that blooms in the blue winter night? I am a wave that, unable to reach the sky, beats its head against the shore.

ihaloka śukhamellām vyārthamāṇenuḷḷa
paramārtham ñān ariññapoḷ
iravum pakalum kaṇṇīr ozhukki
ninne ariyān koticcū... amme
ninne ariyān koticcū

When I came to understand the truth that all worldly comforts are worthless, I shed tears, day and night, longing to know you, Amma.

dukhabhārattāl taḷarunnorenne nī
āśvasippikkān varillē...?
ettīṭumennuḷḷa āśayōṭe ñān
nityavum kāttirikkunnu... amme
nityavum kāttirikkunnu

Won't you come to comfort me, who am weary of the burden of sorrow? With the desire that you will come, I am waiting always, Amma.

Amma's voice again resounded in my ears. "Is it enough to remain a bud? Embrace the pain of flowering. Allow the bud of your heart to blossom. The fragrance and beauty that are to be shared with others are within you. Do not heed those transient growing pains. Prepare for the dawn of the sun of knowledge."

Far better the sorrow that God bestows than happiness from any other quarter. The one who runs after pleasure is apt to turn his back on God. A devotee is one who seeks out grief. To him or her alone the Blissful One belongs. There is depth in suffering. When we are prepared to bear suffering for God's sake, it becomes a tapas. Amma says that life is God's boon to us, not a curse. There is no problem with the world. Problems and weariness are of the human mind. We must learn to get over them. The training for this is spirituality. Our life must become an art.

Some things in this universe can be known only through experience; truth can be realized only experientially. God is a divine experience that can neither be transmitted nor expressed. The boundless love and compassion brimming in Amma help us intuit what God is.

Vision of Divine Beauty

17

Having resigned from the Rāman Research Institute, I hastened to take a train to my hometown. I didn't have the patience to wait for Amma's permission. I realized the truth about the value of each passing day only after meeting Amma. Having realized the great loss I would suffer every moment away from Amma, how could I stay away from her? Until we become conscious of Amma's divine presence within us, her physical proximity is very important. Until the inner Guru awakens, the outer Guru is essential. The toddler who is learning to walk cannot do without the help of its mother's fingertip. I had only just begun to tread the spiritual path. I knew nothing of its perils. The Guru alone can teach us how to turn those obstacles into stepping-stones. For the disciple who has renounced the world and taken refuge at the Guru's feet, there is nothing like an 'obstacle.' All experiences become aids to spiritual growth. The Guru's compassion-filled gaze will lend the disciple the necessary strength. The Guru's presence is truly a plenitude of such powers that are not visible to the eye, even if one has a thousand eyes. Pure hearts will have no difficulty appreciating the endless bhāvas of a Guru. In order to gain such purity of heart, nearness to the Guru's physical presence is necessary.

When I reached home after the train journey, I collapsed in sheer exhaustion. The body was unable to withstand the extreme austerity of forgoing food and sleep for days together. I had to be admitted into a nearby hospital for a few days. Having found symptoms of pneumonia, the doctors prescribed complete bed rest. I had quit my job and rushed here out of an excruciating longing to see Amma, only to end up in a hospital. I tried to console myself with the thought that this was Amma's punishment for having resigned from my job without her permission.

My father went to Vaḷḷickāvu to inform Amma about my predicament. She did not accede to my request to visit her in Vaḷḷickāvu. She told my father that I should not travel for the time being and that she herself would come to the hospital to see me. I had told my father before he left that I would visit Amma in Vaḷḷickāvu and then return immediately to the hospital. This hope did not bear fruit. When Amma expressed willingness to visit me in the hospital, my father protested. "No, Amma, you needn't take the trouble to go all the way there. The doctors said that he will be discharged after two days." Hearing this, Amma gave my father some prasād and ash that she blessed for me. My father smeared the ash all over my body. After partaking of the prasād, I felt much relieved. However, I still felt greatly distressed by the sorrow of not having been able to meet Amma.

I was unable to sleep that night. Months had passed since I last saw Amma. My first meeting with her had been a momentous event that totally changed my outlook on life. I lay in the hospital bed, praying unceasingly to Amma—the Goddess of the Universe who had created a Vaikuṇṭha[21] on earth and enabled thousands

[21] The abode of Lord Vishṇu; here being used figuratively to mean heaven.

of her children to dance in ecstasy—to ensure that I would never become estranged from her again. I tried to sleep but could not.

Suddenly, I felt the soft touch of a cool breeze. I only realized later that the sweet-smelling wind caressing me heralded the arrival of the Divine Mother, the embodiment of compassion. The tinkling sound of the anklets Amma used to wear reached my ears. In one corner of the room, a circle of light seemed to be taking shape. The radiance of Amma's gentle smile permeated that light. The whole building seemed to be rising. I tried to prevent myself from falling by holding on to my bed, but I was unable to move my hands and legs. Suddenly everything became still. I became entranced by such sweet music as I had never heard before, and dissolved into its stream. Amma's bewitching form began moving toward me, as did the luminous halo of light. Transfixed, I gazed unblinkingly at Amma. The enchanting form of Amma adorned with a profusion of ornaments, a rarely seen form, reached me. After sitting down on the bed, she placed my head on her lap and gently caressed it—priceless moments of a divine visitation! Even though I was aware of Amma kissing my head and her hands banishing all the pain from my heart, I remained still, my body having become immobile. When the thought arose that I could not even prostrate before her, she indicated a 'no' through a gesture. Her caresses became the divine cure that erased the karmas of countless lives.

At this time, the door opened and my father walked into the room. He had gone out to get some warm water for the pills I had to take. As my father approached, Amma's form started becoming indistinct and soon disappeared. Thinking that I was asleep, my father shook me and said, "It's time to take the medicine."

I took the medicine and continued lying in bed. I couldn't talk. I had never before had such a lucid darśan before. My eyes, ears and nose were all recounting the story of my experiences from that darśan. These experiences were all pulsations of the infinite beauty Amma has kept hidden inside her. Even though I knew intellectually that Amma is not confined to her body, the knowledge that these experiences bestowed is something words cannot describe. For this reason, I did not try to tell my father anything.

The next day, I insisted on going to Vaḷḷickāvu. The doctor relented at last and discharged me from the hospital, but only after reminding me that I needed to rest for a few more days. Accompanied by my father, I went straight to Amma. She was sitting in front of the kaḷari, as if waiting for me. She didn't look as if she had rested after the previous night's bhāva darśan. The red-sandal mark on her forehead was still intact. She had not changed from the clothes she had worn for bhāva darśan. The ash that had scattered while she gave prasād to the devotees had left white stains on her clothes, hair and face. Even those particles of dust seemed unwilling to leave her. The moment Amma saw me from afar, she beckoned me. I ran to her and prostrated. She lovingly laid me on her lap and caressed me. That divine fragrance I had smelled the day before during darśan in the hospital room I now sensed emanating from Amma's body. Crying for a few minutes in Amma's lap assuaged my grief greatly. It is the relief one feels upon realizing that there is someone to shoulder all our burdens. This relief develops into self-confidence. None but God can bestow on us such self-confidence. I noticed tears of love and compassion welling up in Amma's eyes too.

"Amma, did you come to see me?" I asked.

She nodded her head to indicate a 'yes.'

"Then why did you leave without saying anything?" I probed again.

Amma didn't say anything; she just smiled. The answer to my question was in that smile.

Even speech is an impediment during the moments of divine experience. On such occasions, talking ceases. Silence is the language of the soul. Language is superfluous in the meeting of souls.

The union of the jīvātma and Paramātma heralds the moment of oneness between the Guru and disciple. The disciple becomes a baby before the Guru. When the disciple brims with innocence, the Guru becomes a Mother. Veiling Her endless divine aspects, She binds the disciple with a sweet and endearing motherliness. That bond leads the disciple to eternal freedom and bliss. In order to do this, the Guru uses the bhāva of motherhood to take the disciple to the innocence of infancy.

An infant sees no evil, for there is nothing but goodness in its mind. Its mind is not filled with many thoughts either, only the thought of its mother. Its world is its mother; its faith is in its mother. The words of others cannot rob its faith because it has experienced the love embodied by its mother. It is not interested in anyone else. If it doesn't see its mother, it will cry. That is the only language it knows.

"Is there any prayer greater than crying? If we can cry for God, we don't need anything else to protect ourselves from worldly miseries."

I remembered these words of Amma. While lying on her lap and crying, the 'I' in me was dissolving into nothing.

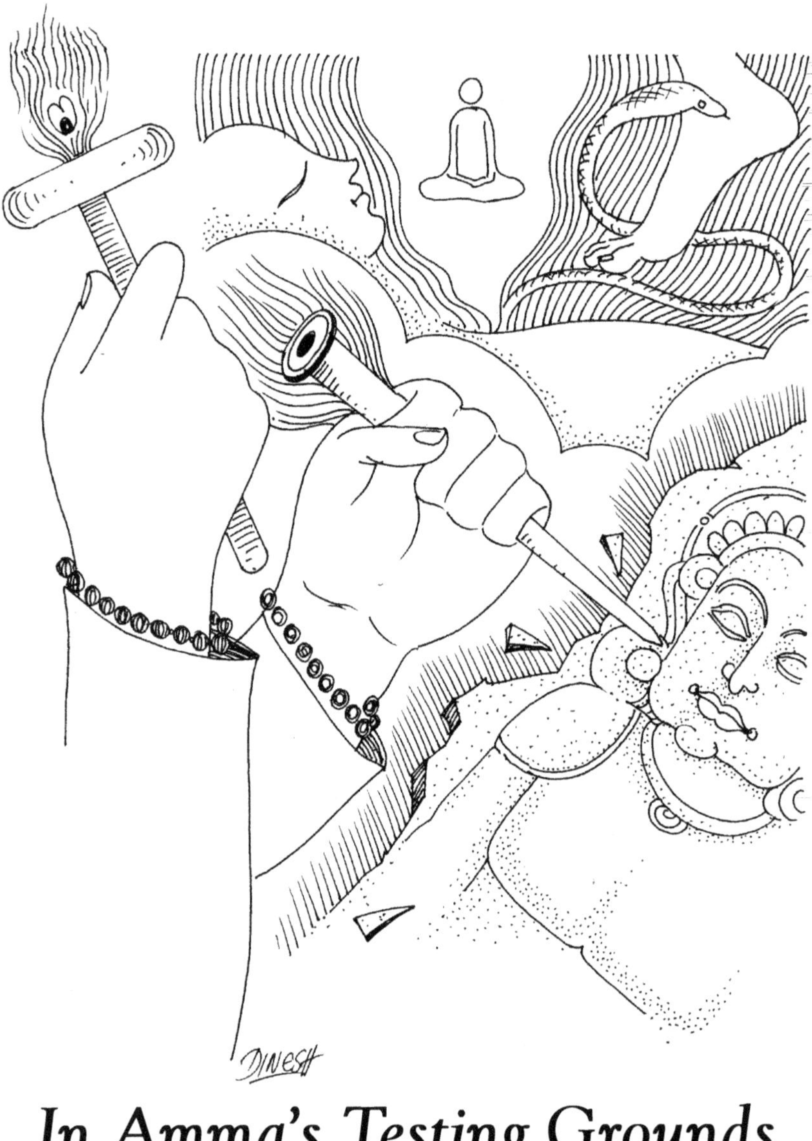

In Amma's Testing Grounds

18

This universe is an emblem of unity—the stars that remain in place because of the power of mutual attraction, the revolving planets, the recondite mysteries that can only be fathomed at the highest levels of meditation. Amma says that there is divine beauty everywhere in the universe. There is no ugliness whatsoever. All perversions are fabrications of the human mind. If one has love, one can perceive beauty anywhere. Through the mesmerizing power of love, one attains the purity needed for beholding the vision of divine beauty. Amma is trying to awaken that divine love within us.

When I returned from Bangalore, I started staying with Amma. I did not face any opposition from my family. The days that followed were a rare opportunity to dedicate my time exclusively to *sādhana*. The dawns that diffused the intoxicating bliss of sādhana, and the dusks that made me cry for no reason, passed swiftly. How much I wanted in those days to spend an entire lifetime crying for

God! I basked in the aura of love emanating from the wondrous phenomenon that is Amma and forgot everything else. When we realize that all we have gained is in fact no gain, we are no longer deluded by those so-called gains. Developing this dispassion isn't easy, but the presence of a great Guru like Amma helps us do so. This change in our outlook on life is what we gain through spirituality. This is the divine experience Amma imparts.

Every moment with Amma was a reminder of how valuable each day was. Day and night equally would impart a festive intoxication. By the time we set out with water vessels at three in the morning, Amma would have already reached the jetty, carrying the biggest water vessel. When asked, she would say she was used to carrying big burdens. I suppose carrying a water vessel isn't so difficult for one who bears the burdens of the world! In those days, one would have to wait a long time to get water from the pipes. This was truly a tapas. There would be no water in the taps in the mornings. Therefore, we would have to collect enough water for the āśram before daybreak. Amma was particular that no devotee coming for darśan should suffer on account of there not being any water. She was teaching us not to waste any opportunity to serve devotees.

At that time, one could count in one hand the number of permanent residents in the āśram. That was before it was registered. There wasn't even a hut then that could be said to represent the āśram. Lying down on the sands in front of the kaḷari and falling asleep while stargazing was meditation indeed. The kaḷari, where Amma used to give darśan, was the only building. The altar in the shrine contained a sword and trident, divine weapons Devi used to uproot the ego and impart wisdom! The ego's existence is annihilated when it comes face to face with love. Amma demonstrates that love can conquer where weapons cannot. Devi's weapons cannot be the sword and trident we see. Amma says they are only symbols. Why would Devi need weapons anyway? When

She who can change anything by mere will-power lives with us, armed with Her invisible weapons, all our doubts and misgivings will end. No mother will take up arms against her children. That being the case, we must consider the weapons in Mother Kāḷi's hands to be love, compassion and other divine virtues. The ego's upraised hood bows down before this love.

Upavāsa

19

IN THE OLD DAYS, the āśram wasn't as crowded as it is today. Amma had more time to spend with the brahmacāris and brahmacāriṇis then, ensuring that we adhered to the prescribed routine and paid attention to our spiritual practices. She wanted us to meditate for eight hours daily. Amma would also come for meditation. She was very particular that everyone should sit together for meditation. We were not supposed to move our bodies or open our eyes. On some days, Amma would arrive with some pebbles that would land on those who were inattentive. This was to make us aware when the mind was straying away from the form of God. Once Amma started meditating, she would open her eyes only hours later. In her presence, it was possible for us also to sit for such a long time. When Amma is near, it is easy to get one-pointed concentration. That's why no one felt that meditation was particularly tough. No matter how busy she was, Amma would check at four in the morning if everyone had woken up, and rouse those who were sleeping. On some days, Amma would spend the night on the veranda outside the meditation room. If even one person did not follow the routine, she would not even drink water that day. No one would mind if Amma scolded him or her, but none could bear it if she went without food and thus inflicted pain on her own body. For this reason, there was usually no lapse in adhering to the routine. Meditation for eight hours, chanting of the *Lalita Sahasranāma*, practice of *Haṭha Yoga* exercises, study of Vedic scriptures and singing of bhajans—these continued without fail.

One day, Amma came into the meditation room and announced, "Children, you must fast and observe silence at least once a week." For the whole day of our fast, we were to remain in the meditation room, meditating and chanting our mantras. Amma chose Saturday for this purpose.

When Saturday arrived, everyone went to sit inside the meditation room and soon became immersed in sādhana. Later that morning, Amma served everyone watered-down milk. Before she left, Amma reminded us all, "No one will get any food today."

When it was eleven, she came in again with an earthen pot. "Children, you shouldn't starve! There's no harm in eating bananas."

She distributed steamed plantains to everyone. She had also brought sweetened coffee for all of us. "Children, don't eat anything else."

With this reminder, Amma left. Everyone became engrossed in meditation and *japa* [repeated chanting of a mantra]. Thereafter, Amma came twice or thrice to the meditation room and checked on us through the window. We did not see her for a long time after that. As instructed by Amma, everyone gazed at the picture of his or her ishṭa devata and strove to visualize that form within.

It was after two in the afternoon. No one had left the room. Amma came to the door and looked inside. Her face looked wan. There were streaks of soot on her face, blouse and skirt, and beads of perspiration on her forehead. She gazed on everyone with an expression of deep compassion. Amma then said, "Children, Amma feels bad. Isn't it because of Amma's words that you children aren't eating? O Lord, how cruel I am! When Amma saw her children's surrender, she couldn't sit still. She went into the kitchen and prepared rice and curries. Amma doesn't have the heart to make her children starve. She felt greatly disturbed. Get up quickly. Amma will serve you all."

Amma called us all and made us eat. A devotee witnessing this scene laughed and said, "The word '*upavāsam*' (the Malayāḷam word for 'fast') means 'to be near the Lord.' Therefore, even if Amma's children eat, they wouldn't have broken their fasts. After all, aren't they near Amma all the time?"

Truly, when one is with the Lord, hunger and thirst vanish. Only when Amma reminded us did we feel like eating. In the coolness of motherly affection, one loses one's body consciousness. How enthusiastically we forwent food and sleep for the sake of getting a vision of the Lord! One cannot be satisfied by material pleasures alone. One can experience divine bliss in this very life. This is possible only through sādhana and the Guru's blessings. Although meditation, japa, good deeds and the observance of vows are all means to attaining divine bliss, the best way is association with mahātmas. In their presence, our mental impurities will be gradually burned away.

Even though the supreme reality is within us, we have a long way to go before realizing it. What in the universe could be closer to us than the soul? We experience the changeless, imperishable, bliss-saturated and omnipotent consciousness in completely different ways, as differently as we see day and night. That is why we cannot realize the Truth without the help of one who has attained knowledge of the Self. Our closeness to Amma is totally unlike any other bond. She mingles with us like an ordinary person in order to lead us to the world of the Self. Her every move is full of meaning.

Pilgrimage to Aruṇācala

20

Amma used to make annual trips to an āśram in Tiruvaṇṇāmalai. It was an āśram that Neal Rosner (now Swāmi Paramātmānanda Puri), an American disciple, had given her. In an old temple there, the day of Kārtika in the month of Vriścika is considered especially auspicious. Devotees from all over India come to Tiruvaṇṇāmalai days before, and stay there in order to see and worship the lamp that is lit on that day, to circumambulate the mountain, and to take part in the chariot festival. Amma would usually arrive the day before the lamp was lit.

Recollections of the first visit with Amma to Tiruvaṇṇāmalai are still fresh in my memory. We went there by train. Needless to say, the journey with Amma was thoroughly enjoyable. She struck people as being like a mischievous kid. Like a bus conductor walking up and down the aisle, asking if everyone had gotten their tickets, Amma would run around asking, "Son, did you get peanuts? Can Amma give you some *avil* [flattened rice grains]? Who hasn't got bananas yet?" From time to time, Amma would sit between passengers and sing bhajans.

The other passengers would stare in amazement at this blouse-and-skirt-clad girl running about. Amma never hesitated to give prasād even to those who were unfamiliar with her. Not only that, she would also sit next to them and exchange pleasantries with them.

Dusk was setting in. I sat gazing at the palm trees disappearing into the Western horizon, which the setting sun had smeared saffron. The vermilion light had also cast its hue on the faces of those in the train. Every one of those ruddy faces was gazing awestruck at Amma. During the evening bhajans, all the passengers joined in enthusiastically. Passengers from other compartments crammed into ours. Some became so mesmerized by the rhythm of the bhajans that they started dancing. When the bhajans ended, some inquired about Amma. Others went up to her and kissed her hands. Yet others stared without blinking at Amma's cherubic face. In those days, not many people had heard about her. However, many devotees from Tamil Nāḍu used to visit Amma in Vaḷḷickāvu. At each railway station, many would be waiting for her, garlands in hands. They would then join us on our journey. What started as a 20-odd group became bigger. At first, there were only brahmacāris and a few householder devotees with Amma. Gradually, the entourage swelled tremendously.

When we reached Tiruvaṇṇāmalai, the devotees who had come to receive Amma had already arrived. Among them was a Parsi devotee known as 'Bhagavān Priya.' She had lived with Ramaṇa Maharshi[22] for 33 years. She welcomed Amma on behalf of the Ramaṇa Āśram and garlanded her. Amma was then ushered into the Ramaṇa Āśram. After bhajans, Amma started giving darśan. A huge crowd quickly formed around Amma.

The next day was the chariot festival in the Tiruvaṇṇāmalai temple. Hundreds of thousands of people would converge there that day. Juggernauts that towered over buildings had been lined up for the festival. Nealu (Neal) insisted that Amma should see the chariot festival. Finally, Amma agreed to go. Nealu had already

---

[22] An enlightened spiritual master (1879 – 1950) who lived in Tiruvaṇṇāmalai in Tamil Nāḍu. He recommended Self-inquiry as the path to Liberation, though he approved a variety of paths and spiritual practices.

arranged a solitary place for Amma and her entourage to see the chariot festival. It was the terrace of a two-story roadside building right next to the temple.

Chariots for the festival filled the temple's inner courtyard. Thousands of people lined up, holding the thick rope they would use to pull the chariot. Nealu and other devotees escorted Amma to the place they had arranged for her. People had already taken their places in shops, on top of walls, inside buildings and on terraces. The sea of humanity swarming ahead did not leave even a hairbreadth of empty space uncovered. The police blew on their whistles to calm the crowds. There was a chance the masses would become unruly once the chariots started moving. The devotees fervently pulling the chariots would forget everything in a state of intoxication. Once the chariots lurched forward, it wouldn't be easy to stop them. That was why the police were trying to clear the devotees off the road to prevent the colossuses from knocking into them. As the crowd was disorderly, the devotees had not started pulling the chariots yet.

All of a sudden, a man emerged from the throng and ran up the terrace. He wore a turban and layers and layers of clothes, and held a fan, giving an impression of outlandishness. As soon as they saw him, people humbly moved out of the way.

Who could that man be? I looked on keenly in amazement.

The luster in the eyes of this man who smiled and strolled across the terrace set him apart as someone out of the ordinary.

Finally, this strangely accoutered man with the fan in hand reached Amma. He was an *avadhūta* known as Rāmsūrat Mahārāj. He had picked Amma out from the masses and run to her. He stood fanning Amma with the fan he had in his hand. She affectionately caressed this yogi as he stood gazing at Amma without blinking. Even though we couldn't understand anything the two of them said in the language of silence, the majesty of that stillness transformed us briefly at least into silent sentinels. We gazed spellbound at the lotus of Amma's face in which the Universal Mother's divine moods blossomed unchecked. After some time, he walked down and disappeared into the sea of humanity. In truth, those of us with Amma forgot all about the chariot festival. This incident reminded us yet again that in Amma's presence, nothing else is important.

Hearing the booming of a cannon, I looked down. The chariots had started moving. The flock of devotees who had forgotten everything in the intoxication of bliss started moving forward. The sight of the police struggling to move people away from the chariots' course added to the excitement of the procession.

Suddenly Amma's manner changed. "I want to leave now!" she insisted stubbornly.

"Where to?" we asked, amazed.

"I don't like standing here."

Nealu and the other devotees were flabbergasted. "Amma, you can't leave now. It will be difficult to leave this place until the chariots have left. The steps leading down and all the roads are choked with people."

However, Amma did not relent, no matter how hard we tried. Shoving us aside, Amma ran down the steps swiftly. When she dashed into that sea of people, she must have inadvertently stepped on many, thus blessing them. We ran after her.

Amma does not have body-consciousness; she is not attached to the body either. The disciples are duty-bound to protect the Guru's body. We joined hands and formed a safety ring around Amma to protect her. However, we were unable to maintain this ring for long. As soon as it was caught in the whirlpool of people, it disintegrated into pieces. Swirling about aimlessly and unable to find a way out, we were washed away by that human river.

We not only did not know where Amma was, the so-called bodyguards who had valiantly formed the safety ring around her were nowhere in sight. As we stood aimlessly, utterly exhausted, a few people came from somewhere in the crowd to our rescue. They were devotees of Amma from Madurai. They pushed open the gate of a house and ushered us inside.

"We have to locate Amma quickly!" I told them.

Hearing this, they laughed. Unable to understand the meaning of their laughter, we looked at each other. "It was Amma herself who sent us to help you," they said. "She is right here!"

That was when we realized that Amma was indeed sitting in the porch of the house! How ironic that Amma had to send forces to help us who had presumed to be her bodyguards. Implicit was the message that Amma does not need anyone's protection.

How had Amma reached this house? None of us were aware that there was a devotee's house in the vicinity. Amma's totally unexpected visit had brought joy and overwhelming bliss to the family staying in the house. We now stood before Amma in tattered rags. When Amma saw the state we were in, she burst out laughing.

"Children, did you get pushed and shoved? Amma got some hard knocks! It was really fun!"

Doesn't the Lord enjoy being pummeled by His devotees? Amma tried to make us laugh by cracking jokes. For her, everything is fun. For those who can enjoy everything, how can there be sorrow? If you praise them, they are happy. If you criticize them, they are even happier! If they win, they are happy. If they lose, they are even happier! If they have material comforts, they are happy. If they have sorrowful experiences, they are even happier! Since mahātmas know how to turn every incident into a blissfully intoxicating incident, who can make them sad?

All those in Amma's entourage who had been dispersed reached the house, one after another. Then some people came in, carrying Nealu.

Nealu, born into a Jewish family in America, told Amma in Malayāḷam, "O my Mother! I think I just died! My ego has been completely crushed! I will never again insist that Amma see the chariot festival!"

Hearing that, Amma started roaring with laughter. The waves of that laughter must have resounded throughout the universe! It seemed so pregnant with meaning.

The Guru's aim is to crush our egos. The Lord has given us all we need. Our only lack is that we don't know all that we need to know. The Guru has come to help us realize this. For this to happen, the layers of the ego must be peeled away, one after the other.

"In any case, Amma should not have run down from the terrace like that," said all those around Amma.

Immediately, Amma's bhāva changed. In a voice that bore the gravitas of Guruhood, she said, "Children, did you really think Amma would stand comfortably above the chaos to watch the chariot festival when there were 10,000 people below struggling to find a place even to stand? I'm not one to enjoy myself when others are suffering."

Her words were like thunderclaps. *How can I enjoy myself when others are suffering?* Amma's words, bearing a priceless message I will never forget for the rest of my life, lapped like waves against the shore of my mind.

Mahātmas can never think about their own happiness. They are personifications of self-sacrifice. If we observe them carefully, we will realize that their lives demonstrate the sweetness of love and the glory of self-sacrifice. Amma is showing us how to do our duties while savoring every moment of life. When our every action becomes an expression of love, it becomes beautiful. Selfless deeds arise from love.

Divine love flows for no reason whatsoever. Every one of our spiritual practices should be done to awaken this divine love. The Guru's hallowed presence infuses the fragrance and coolness of love into a life that is in danger of becoming mechanized, and makes every experience in life a means to attain God.

The Guru is an embodiment of love and self-sacrifice, a lighthouse of wisdom. The great Gurus are like beacons that give a sense of direction to the boats of lives drifting aimlessly in the ocean of samsāra. Through her motherly affection, Amma lends every one of her children strength to rise above Māyā and opens the portals to the path of Liberation.

In the olden days, one would have to wait for years in order to hear anything directly from the Guru. One's patience and sense of renunciation would be tested. It seems the tests in the *gurukulas*[23] of yore were tougher than the entrance examinations for admission into educational institutions today!

Once, a disciple reached a Guru who was sitting with closed eyes, immersed in meditation. He waited until the Guru opened his eyes. He had to wait for years before being blessed to see the Guru's benign gaze. The Guru closed his eyes again only to open them years later. The disciple rejoiced. Minutes after opening them, though, the Guru again closed his eyes and became immersed in meditation. Years passed. The Guru opened his eyes to gaze upon the disciple who was meditating on the Guru's feet. The disciple soared into a state of rapture. The Guru again closed his eyes. The disciple waited patiently. He forgot all about food and sleep. After many years, the Guru opened his eyes again. He embraced the disciple. That embrace culminated in the disciple's Self-realization. All beings in the Guru's presence have a tale to tell, the tale of sacrifice! The ultimate peace that these blessed lives, these living chronicles of love, gain is a divine elixir for liberation from samsāra.

God isn't far away. He is here in the Guru's presence. We don't need to wander any further in search of a Guru. Human life isn't meant to be confined to the waves of the samsāric ocean. If we

[23] Literally, the clan [kula] of the preceptor [Guru]. In the past, students would stay with the Guru in Her hermitage for the entire duration of their studies (a period of about 12 years).

open the eye of love, we will see God everywhere! Apathy and fear will disappear forever. The Guru is like a phenomenon that can transmute base metals into gold. Love transforms the nature of our inner substance totally. When that change happens, we will experience the whole world changing. When the visible universe is devoid of love, it becomes worldly. When it is permeated with love, it becomes God's playfield.

Mountain Circumambulation

The devotees who go to Tiruvaṇṇāmalai for the festival associated with the lighting of the Kārtika lamp also circumambulate the Aruṇācala Mountain. Ramaṇa Maharshi did not see Aruṇācala as a mere mountain, but as the Almighty Himself. Often, he would call out "Father!" and crawl around the whole mountain. Mahātmas behold the Lord even in objects we consider insentient.

In order to circumambulate the mountain fully, one would have to walk a distance of about 12 kilometers. The previous day, we had climbed the mountain and were exhausted as a result. For this reason, no one attempted the mountain circumambulation. That evening, someone came running and said, "Amma is not to be seen!"

We jumped up and started running. As we had received the news rather late, we hired a horse-drawn carriage and started looking for Amma in various places. I recalled something that had taken place while climbing the mountain the previous day. There were many caves in the mountain. Amma had gone into one of them and started meditating. She had not opened her eyes, even after a long time. It was tough rousing Amma from her meditation. Even after she opened her eyes, she hadn't agreed to come out with us. She had only emerged after much coaxing. When she stepped out, Amma had said, "I don't feel like leaving this place at all. I am controlling the urge to remain, by thinking of my children."

We figured Amma had entered some cave. How were we to find her, since there were so many caves in the vast Aruṇācala Mountain? We moved here and there in sheer desperation, searching for Amma. By then, the horse-drawn carriage had reached near Aruṇācala. We must have traveled about five kilometers along the road running around the mountain. That was when we sighted Amma walking some distance away. When we reached near her, we got down from the carriage and ran toward her.

Her fingers were held in a mudra. Her face bore a bewitching smile. Her eyes were half closed. Amma was staggering as she walked. Goddess Pārvati circumambulating Parameśvara—that was how the sight struck me! We started walking with her. The horse-drawn carriage accompanied us. We tried to bring Amma's mind down from its rarefied heights by chanting Vedic mantras. We sang bhajans devoutly at the top of our voices and thus circumambulated the mountain. The chanting of the *praṇava mantra* 'Om,' the chanting of pentasyllabic mantras and the singing of bhajans caused the bliss of devotion to rain down upon us. After walking a long distance, Amma turned around to look at us compassionately. Her gaze had the power to burn to ashes one's karmic burdens and vāsanas! Gradually, Amma came down to our level. She then started joking and making small talk. A little later, Amma sat down under a tree by the roadside. We all huddled around her. After some rest, we resumed walking. No matter how much we insisted, Amma refused to get into the horse-drawn carriage. We walked for about 12 kilometers. At the spot where the circumambulation ends, Amma noticed a snake charmer. He was making the snakes sway with his playing. Like a small child, Amma stood gazing at this sight with utmost curiosity.

"Children, why don't snakes have hands and legs?"

Hearing her question, everyone started laughing. Amma herself gave the answer. "When they had hands and legs, they must have misused them. Children, remember that this may be the fate of such people."

Amma's facial expression changed. The majesty and dignity of the Guru were writ large on her face. She continued, "Children, Amma knows that you don't love anything or anyone more than you love Amma. You cannot think of any other God. Therefore, this circumambulation is not necessary for you. However, society looks up at you as exemplars. Our ancestors were able to see the Lord in the Guru. Not everyone may be able to do so in this age. Therefore, practices like circumambulation are necessary for ordinary people. Society must learn these practices from people like you. Children, you must also set an example by following these practices yourselves. That is why you must honor protocol, to uplift the ordinary people wandering in the forest of transmigration. In order to teach you, Amma had to behave in this way."

Amma said later, "Amma is always scolding her children. You shouldn't be sad, thinking that Amma doesn't love you. It's because Amma is full of love for you that she chides you. Children, you are Amma's wealth. When she renounced everything, she got something she could not renounce—her children! When you become the light for the world, Amma will truly be happy. She doesn't need your praise or service. Gain the strength to shoulder the world's burden of sorrows."

Amma's nectarous words were chastening. We fell at her sacred feet and prayed, "Amma, make us good people. May we be able to sacrifice our lives for the good of the people."

Sagely Simplicity

21

People are usually eager to flaunt their insignificant talents before others, but mahātmas mask their sublime greatness and revel in the world. Occasionally, something overflows from their brimming pots and we take it in, utterly amazed.

"Why do mahātmas hide their glory and act like ordinary souls?" I once overheard a devotee asking Amma this question.

Amma's answer was a counter question. "Why do police officers sometimes disguise themselves during investigations? At times, they may even act like thieves."

I have often felt that Amma is like one of those police officers. She has assumed the human guise solely to bind us with her love. Why should she bind us? To free us from the shackles of all other attachments. To make us eternally free. To help us attain the abode of Peace.

Even though Amma tries hard to conceal her true nature, her efforts do not always succeed, particularly with her children who tail her like a shadow. This is why the āśram residents get numerous opportunities to encounter personally at least a little of Amma's glory.

I remember an incident that took place after I had become an āśram resident. One dawn, when I emerged from the kaḷari after my *arccana* and meditation, I saw Amma seated on the veranda, writing something hurriedly. I slowly walked to where she was.

With one hand, Amma hastily covered what she had been writing. Looking at me, she said, "Son! Don't come here now!" I obeyed.

However, my curiosity was aroused. What could Amma be writing? Let me wait until she has finished, I decided. Over the next few hours, Amma filled up two 80-page notebooks. I went near Amma again and asked, "Amma, what were you writing?"

"Nothing, son."

"Nothing? But I saw you writing furiously, filling up two books!"

Amma merely smiled and said, "I don't remember."

'The events of millions of years gone by rose up within me'—Amma had written this line in a poem she penned years ago. How could someone who could recall everything that had transpired over lifetimes not remember something that took place moments before? My appetite for finding out what Amma had written was whetted!

Without further comment, Amma picked up the books and ran away! I searched everywhere, but could not find her. I knew Amma could become invisible if she chose to. But why had she run away with those books? So what if I read those books? I saw Amma only much later, at dusk. She was lying in the coconut grove, in deep sleep. I searched the whole āśram premises for those books, but couldn't find them. Finally, I gave up the idea of finding them.

Many months passed. Once, while cleaning the hut Amma was staying in, a wooden trunk caught my eye. Ants were coming out of it from all four sides. When I opened it, I saw the books Amma had written. I felt so grateful to the ants for leading me to the books! I picked up the books. When I opened one of them and read the first page, I was stunned! Amma had explained the most recondite and profound mysteries of the universe in surpassingly splendid language. Those lines were brimming with unbelievable poetic beauty. While reading the next page, I became aware that

Amma was walking toward the hut from a distance. I put the books back where they had been.

At that time, a devotee from Trivandrum who used to come to the āśram had recast some of Amma's ambrosial utterances as epigrams. He obtained permission from Amma to publish them. It was to be the first āśram publication. How nice it would be, I mused, if the contents of those books Amma had written could be included in this publication. Let people realize who Amma really is.

I quickly went into the hut, opened the trunk and took the books out. Suddenly, Amma appeared from out of the blue. She snatched both books from my hands. I tried hard to snatch them away from her. Even though I knew there was no way I could defeat the personification of Omnipotence in any wrestling match, I did not later want to regret not having tried to get those books! Having defeated me effortlessly, Amma seized the books from my hands. She tore them into pieces and flung them into the backwaters. However, when Amma tore the books away from me, some pages had remained in my hands. I dashed away with those pages, consoling myself with the thought that I had managed to get at least something! Those pages later appeared under the heading *'Amṛta Upanishad'* in the first edition of the āśram's first publication.

If we read what Amma has sculpted with the expert hands of the divine wordsmith—among other things, of how the soul enters the womb and suffers under the weight of its karmic burden, remembering the sins of the past; how it calls out to God in total surrender; how it comes to earth with a body bearing the burdens of pleasure and pain; and how it roams through life, which is an amalgam of pain and pleasure—it will become clear that Amma is omniscient; no other proof is needed.

'Amṛta Upanishad'

The body is the cause of sorrow. All sorrows are caused by the body, which is nothing but a bundle of sorrows ensuing from the results of karma. We perform every act egoistically, i.e., with the 'I' thought. The ego is born from ignorance. The body is sentient because of association with the effulgent Ātma, like a red-hot piece of iron in contact with fire. The Ātma thinks 'I am the body' because of association with Māya. This misconception is what ensnares all beings in the meshes of samsāra. Because of this, the mind does not reach the path of Liberation. Depending on the balance of meritorious or sinful deeds one performs, one gains a high or low birth. Actions, whether virtuous or not, create a body. Some people, desiring to live in heaven, perform sacrifices and charitable acts deemed virtuous. If they reach heaven after death, they can stay there and enjoy heavenly bliss until the results of their virtuous acts are exhausted. Thereafter, they will fall headlong into the lunar sphere, and from there, they will unite with ice particles and fall on earth. Here, they become edibles like rice grains that, when eaten by human beings, get converted into blood. This becomes a man's semen, which is discharged into a woman's womb. It is immediately enveloped by a sac of membrane and grows. A summary of this process is as follows:

In one day, the semen and blood unite and become an embryo. After five nights, it develops into a blob. After another five days, it becomes a lump of flesh. In another 15 days, tiny drops of blood cover this lump. After the next 25 days, limbs begin to sprout. In three months, the limbs will have joints, and in the fourth month, fingers will appear. Parts such as gums, nails, the generative system, nose, eyes and ears appear in the fifth month. In the sixth month, holes develop in the ears. In the seventh month, the genital organ, umbilicus, arms and mouth develop. In the eighth month, the hair on the head and other parts of the body will start to grow. In the ninth month, the fetus starts moving its hands and legs in the womb. From the fifth month onward, life force will be manifest in the fetus. The essence of the food eaten by the mother is drawn by the umbilical cord placed at the mouth of the uterus and attached to thin vessels that convey the food essence that nourishes the fetus. After the body has become developed and the life force has become fully manifest, the child remembers its past births and thinks, "O God! In how many different wombs I have been born! How many evil acts I have performed! How much wealth I have accumulated through unjust means! In those lives, I never remembered You or chanted Your sacred names. O God! The suffering I am undergoing now is a consequence of all that. When will I be able to get out of this hell? If born again, I will never do anything evil. I will do only virtuous acts within my capacity."

With such elevating thoughts and prayers to the Lord, and on completion of 10 lunar months, the child emerges through the vaginal passage under the pressure of the force of labor. However much loved and cared for by parents, the sorrows of childhood are unbearable. Likewise, it is certain that people suffer miseries in one form or another even in youth and old age. Why expatiate much? The body is only a bag of sorrows. It is because of identification with the body that beings experience pleasure and pain. It is a fact that the sufferings of birth and death are caused by the body. The Ātma is eternal and separate from the gross and subtle bodies. Realizing this truth and giving up love for the body, live as a Knower of Ātma. All ignorance will disappear once you know that the Ātma—ever pure, ever peaceful, imperishable, ever awake, non-partial, beyond all qualities, the one Self of the whole universe, the supreme Brahman—is separate from the phenomenal world of Māya. Bearing this principle in mind, live on earth until all your prārabdha karma is exhausted.

Expressions of Divinity

22

Living with Amma, we get innumerable opportunities to perceive expressions of innocence in her mental and physical deeds. Some years before, a devotee brought a packet of candies. Amma called us all and said, "Come, children, there are some nice candies here." She divided and distributed the candies among us, and then carefully kept the candy wrappers. When we asked her for the wrappers, Amma said, "No, I won't give them to anyone. They are such pretty wrappers. I want all of them!" Some time later, we noticed the wrappers strewn about haphazardly. Indeed, Amma does not keep anything for herself. The sight of the scattered wrappers conveyed the message that everything was for her children.

Sometimes, devotees living far away would invite Amma to their homes. If we happened to pass any river during our trips there, we would stop the vehicle for a swim in the river. In such situations, Amma would dive into the waters and then refuse to come out. When all our entreaties failed, we would go and sit in the vehicle, defeated. Only then would Amma emerge from the river, and that too, with utmost reluctance.

Once, we were traveling by train to a holy spot in Tamil Nāḍu. When the train was passing through a village, Amma suddenly said, "I want to get down immediately!"

The next station was far away, but Amma was insistent and started arguing with us. To our amazement, the train suddenly came to a halt. It was as if the train had responded to a signal from somewhere to stop. At once, Amma jumped out of the train and walked toward a place not too far away and lay down on the ground. We were terribly anxious, as the train would start any time. We pleaded fervently with Amma to get into the train. Her only reply was, "Don't trouble me! Leave me alone. I will not get up from here!"

Finally, seeing no other way, two devotees carried Amma back into the train.

In those days, Amma's physical features were like that of a child. A question often asked in wonder is, "Why are mahātmas so innocent and we so different in nature?"

Is it because of some lack in us? No, it's not because of any lack. In fact, it's because we have too much of certain things; in other words, the ego—the attitude of 'I' and 'mine,' and the attendant likes and dislikes of our personalities. It is this narrow conception of 'I' that creates the impression that we are lacking in something. It is from this sense of lack or incompleteness that desires are born. We forget the fact that we are Whole and Complete because our minds have become covered by the veil of the ego.

What is it that a Guru or mahātma does? The Guru hacks away at the extraneous material in us. I recall the story of a man who was the proprietor of a shop that sold antiques and statues. Once, a friend visited the proprietor. Lovely statues of varied shapes and colors were on display. There was a rough-hewn stone lying on the ground in front of the shop. The friend saw that the statues on display in the shop were very expensive. Pointing to the stone lying on the ground, the friend asked how much the proprietor would sell it for. "Oh, that one?" the proprietor said, as if totally uninterested. "I'd only be too happy to give it to you and see the last of it!" He handed over the stone to his friend at once.

After a few days, the shop's proprietor went to visit his friend. When he saw a glittering statue of Devi in the friend's pūja room, the proprietor was taken aback. "Where did you get this amazing statue?" he asked with great anxiety.

The friend replied, "It was sculpted from the stone lying in front of your shop, which I had taken a few days ago. You must be wondering how that deformed mass of stone could become this splendid idol of God, right?" He continued. "First, I washed away all the dirt from the stone. Then, I chipped away all the excess parts from the stone and then polished it. That's how this beautiful idol came into being."

This is, in fact, what the Guru does. Through a regimen of discipline, She removes the unnecessary vāsanas from our character and brings out the divinity latent in us. We thus attain Wholeness.

However, even if the Guru is near us, we may not get the results we expect. The Guru is like a magnet, a divine lodestone. There are three types of people. Very few are like steel, which becomes magnetized just by being close to the magnet. Even when the original magnet is removed, the steel does not lose its magnetic power but retains it. Such is the first-rate disciple. Such disciples will later become Gurus themselves.

The second group of people is like raw iron; it gets drawn by a magnet. However, once the magnet is removed, the raw iron will lose its magnetic power. Most of us feel extremely drawn to a mahātma, but the moment we move away from the mahātma, we will go back to pursuing material pleasures and other selfish interests, compelled by the force of our vāsanas and desires.

Most people belong to the third category. Such people are like pieces of wood; even being placed right before the magnet that is the mahātma will make no difference. Not only are such people not drawn to mahātmas, they won't be able to see any greatness in them either. We can draw some relief from the fact that, by Amma's grace, we are not of this category.

When steel is placed near a magnet, how does it get magnetized? The close proximity of the magnet causes the atoms in the steel bar to become aligned in the same direction as the atoms in the magnet. If our association with the Guru is to be of any benefit to us, we must realign our bodies, minds and intellects to the goals and advice She has set. We must abrade the mass of ego that blocks our vision of Truth and surrender to the Guru's will.

The human life we have now and the changes that the previous lives have wrought are all aimed at uprooting the ego in us. The Guru or God wants us to draw near, without egoism and pride, and with the innocence of a newborn babe.

I remember an incident that took place many years ago during a Kṛshṇa Bhāva darśan. Amma was awakening the divinity within by singing hymns in praise of Lord Kṛshṇa. The area in front of the kaḷari was massed with devotees laughing and dancing in the intoxication of devotion.

Bhāva darśan started. I was standing near Amma inside the kaḷari, observing everything. It was the perfect opportunity for seeing up close Amma's playful moods and hearing her humorous quips. She was standing with one foot placed on a pedestal—she used to give Kṛshṇa Bhāva darśan while standing. Amma was verily the epitome of a beauty that defied description, her face illumined by an enchanting smile that was like a brilliant, pulsating orb. Devotees would adorn Amma with shimmering robes, a crown and floral garlands. The fear that Amma's mischievously knowing look would pierce the inner recesses of their hearts caused the heads of some to hang low. As the hearts of some took flight to the supreme state of bliss, their eyes conveyed new meanings to tears.

There were two lines of devotees queuing up for darśan. Everyone noticed two young men stealing into the kaḷari, bypassing the queues. Some didn't like it that they were walking right into the kaḷari when there were so many standing in line for darśan. Amma's expression did not change though. Both of them came and stood before her. One of them started speaking.

"Amma, this is my friend. He has been mute from birth. His family members are suffering endlessly. What should we do for him to gain the faculty of speech?"

Amma looked at my face and smiled sweetly. I didn't understand the meaning of her smile. Without saying anything in reply, Amma caressed them both. She gestured to them to sit by the side. They sat down in a corner of the kaḷari. Amma does ask certain devotees to sit and meditate for some time. Amma also told me the same thing a long time ago. On that day, when I went to test her, Amma took a handful of chrysanthemums from a basket and, putting them in my hands, told me to count out 41 flowers. I very carefully started counting them. When I finished counting, I realized that Amma had given me exactly 41 flowers. With the flowers in my hand, I looked at Amma. Laughing, she asked, "Finished counting?"

I replied, "You gave me 41 flowers!" Without saying anything, Amma laughed again.

Later, on many occasions during Kṛshṇa Bhāva darśans, I used to see Amma giving flowers to some devotees and making them count the flowers. I used to be amazed. It was always 41! One day, I asked her, "Amma, don't you know there are exactly 41 flowers? Why then do you ask people to count?"

"Son, if they are not given some task, they would think about something else. I ask them to do this so that they won't think of other things while they are here at least. Isn't it the case that the mind starts wandering when we are idle? Let the mind dwell on the flowers. May the heart become soft like a flower. May the flower of the heart blossom, spreading its fragrance."

I realized there were a thousand meanings behind Amma's every action. There is so much to learn from her every move. I became aware that what the Guru imparts is what cannot be taught.

After sitting for a short while, the legs of the youths must have started aching, for I saw them getting up slowly and leaving. When they had gone outside, Amma said, "Son, those who just left came to test me. That man is no mute. He was pretending!"

"Amma, you could have told them so! Otherwise, won't they think that you are unable to make out such matters?"

Hearing my outburst, Amma smiled. "Son, what is it to us if they think so? Let them be. After all, didn't they take pains to come here? Let them rejoice, thinking they have won. Why should we take away the joys of others?"

"Wouldn't that make them even more egoistic?"

Hearing my question, I noticed Amma's expression changing. "Son, if they become egoistic, nature will take up arms to crush them."

I did not try to say anything else. Those were the words of omniscience.

Two days later, a postcard addressed to Amma arrived. The following words were written on it:

> "Child, you may recall us. I am the person who brought the mute to you that day. Actually, he is no mute. Child, we came there to see if you could figure this out. We are rationalists. The fact that you could not see through us is proof that you possess no special power. My dear girl, it would be good if you stopped all this and did something else instead!"

I ran to Amma with this utterly derisive letter in hand. Handing it to her, I said, "Amma, please read this letter."

Amma read the letter and laughed out loud. I said, "What do you think now? Didn't I tell you then that they would mock you? Amma, you should have told them then and there! Haven't they gained the upper hand now?"

Hearing my words, Amma started laughing again. She said, "Son, don't be upset. They will come here again."

A few days later, a big group of people arrived at the āśram. The two young men who had come earlier were there too. I asked them straight off if they had come to test Amma again.

"Not at all! We need to see Amma urgently to beg her forgiveness. That's why we've come."

Hearing these words uttered by the friend of the 'mute,' I asked, "What happened that you should feel this way now?"

"I'll make a clean breast of everything. I shall confess everything before Amma."

Feeling the slightest trace of doubt, I looked carefully at him. When I saw the expression on his face, I realized he was greatly troubled on account of something. When Amma was informed about their arrival, she immediately called for them. All of them trooped into the hut and sat down. They started pouring out their troubles to Amma. The man who had come earlier spoke.

"We are students of M.S.M. College in Kāyāmkuḷam. We came here some days ago. When we came to Amma for darśan, one of us pretended to be dumb. We know what we did was wrong. Nevertheless, we did what we did. Now, my friend has really been struck dumb! I am feeling extremely distressed. I took him to many doctors. All of them said that there was no problem whatsoever. When I informed his family members, they too took him to various people, in vain. Finally, an expert in astrological calculations said, 'He has incurred the displeasure of some person in a holy place. Only if he goes to that place and atones for his sin will he regain the faculty of speech.' That's why we have come again with our family members. Amma, you must help him."

Amma hugged the person who had become dumb. She placed his head on her lap and consoled him. She pressed a finger on the man's tongue and closed her eyes for some time. She then made him drink some consecrated water. Amma then encouraged him to say the words 'Amma' and 'Acchan.' He stuttered, trying hard to say those words. After a few moments, he was able to speak again! Calling out "Amma!" he broke down crying. Tears welled up in the eyes of all those witnessing this scene.

In unison, the family members begged Amma to forgive their children for the mistake they had committed. She said, "Amma never ever wanted anything bad to befall these children. However, God is watching everything we do. We must remember that nature has a thousand eyes and ears. Therefore, we should be careful before saying or doing anything. Do not utter meaningless words. Do not idle your time away. Life is very precious. Every moment is priceless. Know that this body that God has blessed us with is a medium for performing good deeds. Our words should console others. That's why God has given us a tongue. Do not use it to ridicule or hurt others. Our every act should be a noble deed. Through good thoughts and good deeds, we should make our precious human lives a worship of God."

Amma's nectarous words created an amazing transformation in them. All of them kept returning to see her. Having perceived new horizons in life, they surrendered themselves at Amma's sacred feet, with the firm resolve to dedicate their lives for the good of society.

In Mumbai Metropolis

23

While engaged in sādhana in Amma's divine presence, I had to leave the āśram yet again. My father had procured for me a good job in Mumbai (Bombay). Amma also insisted that I should go out and work for some time. When one has been in close physical proximity with Amma for some time, how can one leave her and stay far away? I had no choice but to tell her that I would not do so. Amma was, however, of the view that, since I had obtained permission from my father and mother to follow the spiritual path, I was obliged to work for their sake. Conceding to the logic, I agreed to go and work. However, I insisted that I wanted to feel Amma's proximity just as I was feeling it then; if not, I gave Amma fair warning that I would return, as I earlier had from Bangalore. Amma reassured me that she would always be with me.

I arrived in the great city of Mumbai. When I thought about how Amma had decided to sacrifice my life yet again on the altar of materialism, I cried. I was fortunate to find a place to stay at the premises of Sāndīpani Sādhanālaya, a spiritual organization, from where I could go to work. My work place was far away. If I went by bus, I would have to travel for about one-and-a-half hours; by train, for half an hour. I opted to take the bus. The trains were crowded. Often, one would have to be as agile as an acrobat to get into one of the trains. For someone from a place like Kerala, this would have been quite an adventure! The buses, on the other hand, were not crowded. One would get plenty of time to chant one's mantra. As there were many traffic stops, it would take a long time to reach one's destination. This is why most people traveled by train.

The very first bus trip proved to be amazing. When I boarded the bus, I saw that most of the seats were unoccupied. With *māla* beads (rosary) in hand, I sat in one of the empty seats. I felt comforted by the fact that I could now immerse myself in chanting my mantra. Visualizing Amma, I started chanting.

At the next bus stop, a young woman boarded the bus and sat next to me. I didn't like it that she was sitting next to me when so many other seats were unoccupied. Not only that, she sat leaning against me, as if intent on being a hindrance to my chanting.

I began to wonder why she was sitting there and troubling me. Most of the seats were empty. Why was she so keen on sitting next to me when she could have sat somewhere else? While I was pondering over these matters, she looked at me and smiled. I did not return the smile. I started looking out through the windowpane and squeezed myself into a corner. She edged even closer to me! Glaring at her with utmost loathing, I got up and sat in an empty seat at the front of the bus.

After some time, the woman came and sat in front of me, on a seat facing me. Earlier, I could only see her if I turned my head. Now, she was sitting right in front of me! Even if I looked elsewhere, she would remain visible. She had no doubt sat here with that in mind. I had to look down to avoid seeing her. But how long could one sit like that? A short while later, I stood up and walked to the rear of the bus and sat in one of the seats there. Fortunately, the woman didn't come there, though she did seem to be looking at me from time to time. To avoid her gaze, I closed my eyes.

As I had been traveling the day before, I was very tired and fell asleep almost immediately. I dreamt that Amma came and sat next to me. She embraced me with utmost love and affection. I lay my head on her shoulders and cried for a long time. Amma caressed me and kept trying to console me. She kept saying repeatedly that she was with me. When the traffic signal turned red, the bus suddenly braked. Everyone in the bus was jolted. When I opened my eyes, I was shocked; my head was reclining on someone's shoulder! When I realized that it was the shoulder of the woman who had earlier sat next to me, I jumped! She was smiling at me even then. When I saw that smile, I turned pale. Not knowing what to do, I stood petrified, like a statue. The commuters in the bus were staring at me. No one was looking at that woman. They did not even seem to have noticed her. When the bus halted at the next stop, I jumped off the bus. I then took a taxi to work.

The next day, I wrote a letter to Amma.

> "Amma, Mumbai city is not conducive for *sādhaks* in any way. The women here are not right at all! Amma, is this what you meant when you said you would be with me? My spiritual practices are being frustrated. Amma, I'm not experiencing your presence at all. If this is how it's going to be, I'll have no choice but to return soon."

A few days later, I got a reply from Amma.

> "Darling son, Amma came to see you, but you did not pay any attention at all to her. Even when Amma smiled at you, you didn't return the smile. Amma tried to talk to you but you didn't give her a chance to speak. When Amma came near you, you got up and left. Son, don't feel bad about this. Amma will come to you again."

I was stunned! I recalled the incident on the bus. I had personally supplicated Amma to stay close to me. However, not realizing that it was Amma who had come, I had ignored her; behaved contemptuously, rather. Realizing my folly, I broke down and cried.

While traveling the next day, I sat with rapt attentiveness. I scrutinized every person who boarded at every stop. No one sat next to me. Like the *gopis* who waited for Lord Kṛshṇa to steal curd from them, I sat waiting for Amma, with a place for her reserved next to me. No one came that day. I forgot to chant my mantra, and was fully engaged in watching the women who boarded the bus.

The next day, a dark-skinned woman came and sat next to me. I had no doubt whatsoever that it was Amma! I gazed intently at her face but she did not take notice at all. I tried smiling at her. Even though she noticed, she did not smile.

"O Amma, you're acting so well! Don't think you can fool me." I kept mentally voicing these thoughts. I looked at her again and smiled. When there was no response, I asked her, "Are you Malayāḷī?"

"Yes," she replied.

Gathering up courage, I asked, "Are you Amma?"

When I saw the expression on her face, I realized that she had misunderstood the question. Thinking that I had asked if she was married and a mother, she replied, "I'm not married."

"Where in Kerala are you from?" I humbly probed.

"Pālakkāḍ," came the reply.

I introduced myself and explained the reason for my questions. "I have a Guru who comes in various forms and makes mischief to test me. I have no idea when and where she will appear. I wanted to know whether you were my Guru in disguise; that's why I asked you those questions. If I have troubled you, please forgive me."

Hearing my words, the woman, who had a grave demeanor, couldn't help laughing.

The next day, I wrote to Amma again, detailing the experiences during my bus journeys.

> "I had renounced worldly life and taken refuge at your holy feet. Nonetheless, Amma, you, who are the embodiment of compassion, pushed me into the middle of worldliness. I tried to totally distance myself from women, but today, I am going after women. My eyes are on them to see if they are Amma!"

Amma's letter came a few days later.

> "Son, you are not far away from me. You cannot distance yourself from me even if you want to. Son, did you think I had sent you to Mumbai to work in an office and earn money? Never! It was to change your outlook on the world. Son, Amma knows that you love her and she loves you dearly too. However, Amma is not confined to this body. Right now, you are seeking Amma everywhere. What you are looking for in women is only Amma. All women have become Amma for you. Therefore, everything you do has become a sādhana. Your actions can in no way be considered worldly. Son, you will never again get an opportunity like this to train yourself to see all women as mothers. This separation is a blessing in disguise. Son, before long, Amma will call you back again to her. Don't feel sad."

I read Amma's letter over and over again. My eyes brimmed with tears. Are there no limits to the love of Jaganmāta, the Mother of the World? I even wondered if I was deserving of such a great fortune.

My days in Mumbai thereafter presented me with totally different experiences, experiences that spurred me on in spiritual life. I started to feel Amma's love flowing from the office, from where I was staying and even from the streets. Where is God not? Everyone was showering me with love.

There were many days when I cried, seeing the setting sun. I wrote the poem *'Āzhikuḷḷil dinakaran maraññu'* ['The sun has disappeared into the sea'] while sitting on the seashore. It had simply flowed out on the day I arrived in Mumbai. Seeing the setting sun, I imagined it to be the expression of the pining jīvātma's yearning to dissolve in the Paramātma, and this longing took the form of a poem:

āzhikkuḷḷil dinakaran maraññu
aṇayunna pakalil tengaluyarnnu
viśvaśilppiyuḍe vikṛtikaḷḷalle
vishādamentinu naḷinangaḷe
vishādamentinu naḷinangaḷe

The sun has disappeared into the sea.
The dying day has started its lament.
Isn't it all the play of the universal architect?
O lotuses, why this despondency?
O lotuses, why this despondency?

akhilāṇḍarājante vinodarangam
ī lokam śoka pūrṇam
kaḷimarappāvayāy ñānum karayuvān
kaṇṇunirillātta śilayāy

This is the playfield of the sovereign ruler.
This world is full of sorrow.
Like a puppet, I too
Have become devoid of tears, like a statue.

verpāḍin vedana uḷḷilotukki
tīnāḷamāy eriyunnu enmanam
tīnāḷamāy eriyunnu
tīrādukha kaḍaḷin naḍuvil
tīram kānātalayunnu

Suppressing within the pain of separation,
My mind is being scorched by flames,
Scorched by flames.
Amid the sea of endless suffering
I flounder, unable to see the shore.

However, Amma, the sun of knowledge, is rising everywhere, dispelling the dark shadows of sorrow. The sun never sets. Night is not real. For one who traverses outer space, there is neither sunrise nor sunset. In order to experience this, one must reach the zenith, the summit of spirituality! Amma is showering the elixir of divine bliss, which is beyond joy and sorrow, thus removing the darkness within.

Through various experiences, Amma was teaching me the truth that spirituality and materialism were not two. Everything is divine! We should strive to imagine every object as God Himself. The powerful ideas of our minds can lead us to the Truth. We can tap into divine power in anything, but first, we must gain the requisite inner purity. We must purify the heart through noble thoughts, good deeds, prayer, japa, meditation and such spiritual practices. We can experience and realize God, who illumines every object.

Everyone in this world has different experiences. The mental constitution of one person is different from that of another. This is why everyone sees the world differently. Only mahājñānis see the world as it really is. When the mind becomes pure, true vision becomes easy.

* * *

In the days that followed, I became aware that Amma's divine presence was everywhere. Wherever I went, whenever I needed help, someone would rush to my aid. I had been avoiding traveling by train as it was crowded. It would have been difficult to do japa in that hustle and bustle. However, so many people were putting up with the discomforts of train travel. Thinking about my own comfort did not seem right. I resolved to get used to traveling by rail.

The first few days were really difficult. Gradually, I became reconciled to the difficulties. I became used to chanting the mantra while pressed in on all sides by commuters. I recalled Amma's advice that there was no need to set aside any time in particular for the remembrance of God. If one could do spiritual practices even in adverse situations, one would get rewarded more for it. Every letter Amma sent was redolent with the sweet fragrance of love and affection. The satisfaction one gets from sacrificing cannot be obtained from sensual pleasures.

One day, when I boarded the train, the strains of bhajans issuing from the next compartment drew me there. My parched heart had been thirsting to hear devotional hymns, and the vibrations of those songs were like a proverbial shower of nectar. The sight that met me there gladdened my heart. Many people were seated on the floor, singing bhajans. In front of them was a garland-wreathed picture of Durga. Members of the bhajan troupe were singing in abandon, oblivious to everything else. Others were dancing to the tune. These people had found the time to remember God even in this crowd. They were all office workers. That day, I did not notice the passing of time at all. From that day onward, I would board the compartment where the bhajans took place. To distinguish their compartment from the others, the members of the bhajan team would tie garlands outside, on the windows. Seeing the garlands, I would run to board that compartment.

One day, the bhajans ended when the train stopped at the last station. This was where most people got off. While alighting,

I was accosted by the leader of the bhajan group. He introduced himself as Śāntārām. He talked as we walked together.

"I've been meaning to talk to you for a few days; it's only now that I've gotten the opportunity. I feel drawn to you. I've been watching you during bhajans and have seen tears flowing from your eyes. To be able to cry while remembering God is a great blessing. I'd like to get to know you."

I merely smiled, and did not say anything. The feeling of rapture I felt from hearing the bhajans had not ebbed away yet. I was trying to quell the waves of bliss rising within me. After repeated prodding, I introduced myself. About the bliss one experiences while crying to God, I said, "When I think of the love of Jagadīśvari, I cannot help crying again and again."

I don't know whether he understood what I meant. He expressed a desire to learn more about me. Śāntārām and I walked for a long distance. Apart from Amma, I had nothing else to talk about. "You're not working on Sunday, right? Would you mind coming to my place?"

I could not turn down Śāntārām's loving invitation. I told him I would come, and took down the address of the flat where he was staying.

On Sunday, I left for Śāntārām's house. It was not difficult to locate his Andheri apartment. I figured that it was Amma's will that I go there. When I reached Śāntārām's flat, I was surprised. There were only two rooms in the flat, and one of them had been converted into a pūja room. When I saw a photo of Amma meditating amid the pictures of various deities, I was astonished.

"Where did you get this picture?" I asked him.

"There's a story behind that." I noticed the expression on Śāntārām's face changing. We sat down in the pūja room and continued talking.

Although he had had a fairly good job in a private company, Śāntārām was known as a singer. His income was also mainly from singing assignments. Even though he was working, he would take days off for these gigs. The goal of his life was to make money, but no matter how much he earned, it was never enough. Whenever he made some money, he would get together with his friends. Those were the days when he frittered away all his cash, drinking with his friends. God did not take too long to impose a harsh sentence on this man who had become blinded by his ego. It was not punishment. As Śāntārām later realized, it was a saving grace.

After some time, Śāntārām found himself unable to sing. A persistent bad cough proved to be an obstacle to singing. When talking also became difficult, Śāntārām consulted a doctor. He visited various hospitals, but no one was able to diagnose the problem. Many of the medicines he took only caused his health to deteriorate further. A *sanyāsi* told him that his disease had been caused by bad deeds, and that he should atone for them by going on a pilgrimage and donating to the poor. In accordance with this advice, Śāntārām visited many temples and holy places. He also did good deeds like feeding the poor.

In due course, he reached Madurai Mīnākshi temple in Tamil Nāḍu. He entered a flower shop to buy a garland for offering at the temple. In that shop, located right in front of the Mīnākshi temple, he saw a girl rapidly stringing a garland. Next to her was a photo of a woman meditating. This photo was adorned with a garland. Śāntārām asked her who that woman was. The girl said that it was Madurai Mīnākshi Herself. Even after he returned to where he was staying, he was still thinking about that picture. When he lay down, sleep eluded Śāntārām. For a long time, he paced his room. Finally, he fell asleep at daybreak. Śāntārām felt as if the woman he had seen in that picture was hugging him and lovingly caressing his throat. He got up with a start. There was a peculiar fragrance in the room. Wonder of wonders, the alteration in his voice and the cough that had been afflicting him for years had totally disappeared!

He sat down before the altar and tried singing for a long time. There was no problem whatsoever. He quickly ran to the flower shop. There, he saw the girl lighting a lamp before the picture. He asked how she had come by the picture of that woman. The girl replied that a man who had come to buy a garland had given it to her. All he had said was that it was a photo of 'Amma.' He did not know who this 'Amma' was either. Śāntārām wanted that picture. However, she was not prepared to part with it though he asked; ever since she got the photo, her life had become blessed in so many ways.

After two weeks, Śāntārām returned to Mumbai. When he reached home, his wife presented him with a wrapped parcel. A woman had entrusted her with it, asking her to give it to Śāntārām. He unwrapped the parcel. It was the picture from the flower shop! He was stunned! He had wanted it so much. God had delivered it to his house. Śāntārām immediately installed it in the pūja room and began worshipping it.

I listened in silence to Śāntārām's story. What amazed me was that it was a photo of Amma I had taken! This fact astounded everyone. I narrated to everyone the story of how difficult it had been to take that photo.

Many devotees had started clamoring for a photo of Amma meditating. I was the āśram's photographer then. However, Amma did not like having her photo taken one bit. Nevertheless, I requested Amma one day, "Amma, you must allow us to take a photo of you." Amma conceded. I took many photos. However, when the photos were developed, there was nothing! I felt terribly hurt. I had heard that all those who had tried taking Amma's picture had met with the same results.

Once, a professional photographer from Australia tried many times to take a photo of Amma. Every time he tried, the film would get stuck in the camera. The shutter of another photographer's camera stopped working. Whereas these people had tried to take

Amma's photo without asking for her permission, I had taken the photos only after obtaining permission. I made known my chagrin to Amma. Eventually, she let me take a photo of her while she was meditating. It was the photo that I took while she was meditating that Śāntārām saw in the flower shop (photo on page 177). An enlarged copy of that photo had been printed in Madurai. Śāntārām had obtained a copy of that photo. All this struck Śāntārām, who had been pining to know more about Amma, as divinely ordained.

* * *

Every day I spent in Mumbai was changing my outlook on life. The days that passed became a sādhana. The drive to achieve, apparent in the faces of the teeming thousands in Mumbai metropolis, caught my eye. I realized that it was dissatisfaction alone that enlivened the face of modern man, toiling day and night, longing with all his heart to achieve something.

What lends beauty to life is contentment of the heart. This contentment is also the most difficult thing to achieve. The bliss arising from Self-contentment is the very nature of human beings. That is why humans thirst for bliss. We do every action with the expectation that it will give us happiness and satisfaction. However, no material gain is going to give us ever-lasting contentment. The haves and the have-nots are equally discontented. The discontented millionaires! The disaffected lucky ones! The disgruntled handsome and pretty ones! And more than them, those human titans who have got all they desire in life and yet live in unease.

A king may not attain the satisfaction even a beggar gets. For a king to be contented, he would need to rise to the status of an emperor, a king among kings. However, even if he is crowned emperor, the reasons for discontentment will recur yet again in his life. Only knowers of the Self, or mahātmas, like Amma know the ecstasy of Self-contentment. They are like butterflies. Butterflies sip nectar from flowers, but they do not save it up for later consumption. They flutter from flower to flower, sipping nectar, without hurting the flowers, disfiguring their beauty, or blotting out their fragrance. A mahātma doesn't keep anything for herself. Like the butterfly, she accepts just enough for her needs. The presence of enlightened beings enhances the beauty of this world. Theirs is the beauty of supreme knowledge and utter selflessness. Only through renunciation can one gain this beauty.

Once, a king saw a yogi immersed in meditation by a roadside. He felt a desire to accommodate the yogi in his palace. He expressed his desire to the yogi, who accepted the invitation at once. The king was surprised; he had imagined he would have to try very hard to persuade the yogi. The fact that the yogi had accepted the invitation with great happiness caused some misgivings to arise in the king's mind. There was no way the yogi could be a mahātma. If he were, would he have been ready to come, lured by the pleasures of palace life? He corrected the impression he had had of the divinity of the yogi, and returned with the yogi to his palace, which was fitted with every kind of creature comfort. After many days, the king decided to voice his doubts to the yogi.

He went before the yogi and with all humility said, "Your Holiness, I had thought you were a mahātma, but as soon as I invited you to the palace, you were ready to come. This created some doubts. These doubts have started becoming stronger. Are you really a yogi? You are now living in this palace, enjoying all creature comforts. I too am living like that. What then is the difference between the two of us?"

The yogi replied, "In order to learn the answer, we need to leave the palace. Come with me."

With those words, the yogi started walking. The king followed. After they had covered some distance, the yogi told the king, "O king! I never retract a footstep. Therefore, I am not returning to the palace. If you wish, you may come with me."

When he heard this, the king was shocked. "How can I come? I cannot forget my responsibilities just to come with you."

Laughing, the yogi said, "Yes, I know. You cannot come. This is the difference between the two of us. For me, there is no difference between spending my days in a palace and walking through this dirty ditch. I am ever free. Nothing binds me."

With those words, the yogi started moving ahead. The king realized how foolish he had been. Even though he tried to persuade the yogi to return, the yogi continued walking ahead, without so much as turning around to look.

God has given us a body. To quote Amma, "This body is God's gift to us. It is filled with mysteries and wonders. In truth, we are not aware of the workings going on within the body. The wondrous processes involved in transforming the food we eat into blood are going on within. The machine that this body is has auto-healing properties. As far as the scientist is concerned, the chemicals found in the body are worth a few paltry rupees. However, a scientist will not be able to recreate a human by combining these chemicals. This body is constituted of five elements: *ākāś* [ether], *vāyu* [air], *agni* [fire], *jalam* [water] and *pṛthvi* [earth]. Everything found in the external world is found inside us as well. One could say that each one of us is a microcosm of the universe. For this reason, the ṛshis could gain knowledge of the material world through introspection. Invaluable though this body is, it later becomes the cause of untold pain and suffering that assault us when we live without knowing how to use the body, mind and intellect. This body is the medium for God-realization."

We need to observe certain disciplines in our lives. We must strive to purify the body. We are also obliged to maintain its health. It is a tool for doing good deeds. The body falls ill when we treat it badly. A personal regimen is necessary for purifying the mind. The tongue especially needs to be controlled. Our words must be pleasing. We must give the tongue opportunities for singing the glories of the Lord. We should never utter anything idly. Every word that issues from our mouths should be consoling to others. We need the help of the body in order to transcend the level of experience to the realm of understanding.

Once, a scientist conducted an experiment. He divided a glass case with a glass partition. In one side, he put a big fish and, in the other, he put a small fish on which it usually preyed. The big fish tried many times to catch the small fish. Every time, it would come up hard against the glass partition. This must have pained it considerably, for it later ceased its attempts to catch the small fish. Even when the glass partition was removed, the fish never even tried to move to where the small fish was. It imagined there was still a transparent partition there. It had learned a few lessons from experience. It was not easy to unlearn these lessons.

Similar is the case with human beings. Actually, the experiences that humans have gained from the world are as untrue as the experience of the man who sees a snake in a rope. Those who live giving undue importance to the experiences of the world can never tear the transparent veil to behold their true nature. They are not brave enough. Spirituality is only for the courageous. Only the intrepid can cross over to the other realm. What needs to be sacrificed here is the ego-driven life.

Man in the Age of Machines

24

"Son, this is the age of machines"—Amma's words came to mind.

Man has become like a machine. Machines do better work than human beings, and in the field of modern medicine, robots can perform even surgical operations. However, machines cannot love. They cannot understand the pain of others.

In Mumbai's fast-paced life, people work like machines; human beings have become mechanized. Each one thinks only of his or her personal matters. I once saw people walk past a man who had collapsed on the pavement from fatigue, pretending not to have seen him. Some gave him one look before walking straight past. Human lives are considered to have no value! This would never happen in a village. If one fell on the wayside, someone or other would rush to help. I went near the man; he was barely breathing. He gestured for some water, and I poured some into his mouth.

When I saw that man, I recalled Amma's words. "One should feel sympathy for fellow beings. Compassion toward the poor and suffering is our duty toward God. Never miss any opportunity to do good deeds. Consoling those in pain is nothing but worship of the Lord."

When the man had finished drinking the water, he started speaking. When I learned that he had not eaten for days, I bought some food from a nearby restaurant and gave it to him. When I left the old man, I could not help noticing the glitter in his eyes. I felt Amma's loving compassion flowing from those eyes. "Satisfaction lies not in taking but in giving"—Amma's words echoed in my ears.

I realized that everything I had considered meaningless was replete with a thousand meanings. Life has to be meaningful. This is not possible for those who live selfishly. If we realize that Amma is all pervading, what else can we do but love and revere all? I have noticed that when we imagine others as Amma, even those who are selfish will change their attitudes.

Even after I had returned home from work, I could not forget the picture of the old man lying by the roadside. I recalled his gaunt frame; the scene of him, with his hollowed out eyes, begging for water, kept returning to my mind. How many there are in this world who push on through life, enduring such difficulties! How many suffer without means for even one meal a day! When I thought about all this, I did not feel like eating anything that night. I decided to observe a vow of fasting for a few days.

Every person has her problems, problems galore. Where then is the time to lend an ear to the woes of someone else? When I sat in silence at night, immersed in meditation, I experienced Amma coming near and caressing me. "Where there is love, there is no distance"—Amma's words literally came true and, listening to her lullaby, I fell into a swoon. The pain of separation became a divine experience.

The fast was to begin the next day. However, on the very first day, I had to break my fast. It would be more correct to say that Amma made me break my fast. She worked through one Bālakṛshṇan, who was working in my office. Bālakṛshṇan was from Pālakkāḍ, but he had been staying in Mumbai for many years. Although he was about 70 years old, he worked with more zeal than young people. His jokes would relieve the tedium of office work. I used to tell him stories about Amma, but Bālakṛshṇan, who hailed from the Tamil Brāhmin community, was not very interested in hearing about Amma, who was of the fishermen's caste. However, I was going through a phase in which I couldn't stop talking about Amma. If I had anything to say, it would only be about Amma. I would relate stories about Amma without looking to see if Bālakṛshṇan liked them or not. Although he would listen attentively to these stories, he did not have faith in them.

On that day, Bālakṛshṇan came with two packets of rice. He came straight to me and asked, "Have you decided not to eat anything?"

His question caught me by surprise. I had not told anyone about my vow of fasting! How did he know?

"Are you fasting?"

Hearing the question again, I was roused from my reveries. "Yes," I replied, and I noticed amazement dawning on his face.

Bālakṛshṇan then told me about a dream he had had the night before. He had seen Vaḷḷickāvu Amma in his dream! To see mahātmas even in dreams is a great blessing. And this was no mere dream, it was a *svapna darśan*, a divine visitation in a dream. In that dream, Amma had not only informed Bālakṛshṇan about my intention to fast, but also instructed him to insist that I eat! Truly, it is Amma who gets everything done.

Since the food Bālakṛshṇan had brought was in accordance with Amma's desire, I could not abstain from eating. In this way, Amma established herself permanently in Bālakṛshṇan's heart. He began to desire earnestly to meet Amma. I had earlier showed him the photo of Amma I had. That was how Bālakṛshṇan knew that the form he had seen in the dream was indeed that of Amma. Thereafter, he became more interested in hearing stories about her.

It was only later that I learned there was more to the life of Bālakṛshṇan, who was always cracking jokes; there was another side, a sorrowful one. He had lost both wealth and health, and had to bear the family burden, even at that old age. Amma's entry into his heart became a huge blessing. Bālakṛshṇan, whom I had thought a disbeliever, developed great bhakti toward Amma. He surrendered all his problems to Amma. Thereafter, he was reunited with his children, who had left him after a quarrel. I saw him rejoice in the exhilaration of reuniting with his estranged family members.

Why do human beings have to suffer so much? When will all these sufferings end? If we are blessed with the darśan of mahātmas during this woeful journey of life, all our troubles will cease. The Guru is waiting to shoulder the burden of our sins. God is trying, through the form of the Guru, to uplift us from the abyss of life's sorrows.

Sorrow is unreal. We suffer because we desire. No one likes to suffer; everyone wants to be free of suffering. And yet, we continue to desire, and thus our sorrows increase. If we can understand the idiosyncrasies of the mind, we can eliminate suffering. The mind is constantly craving. It abides in endless discontent. Nothing satisfies it. Even if it gets what it wants, it remains unsatisfied. Although the craving for an object lessens when it has been obtained, a new craving sprouts in its place. Mahātmas tell the world, "People suffer because they desire. Desires are the seeds of suffering. When they are gone, one may experience bliss."

The photo the author took and which he later saw in Śāntārām's house (story on pages 165 – 167).

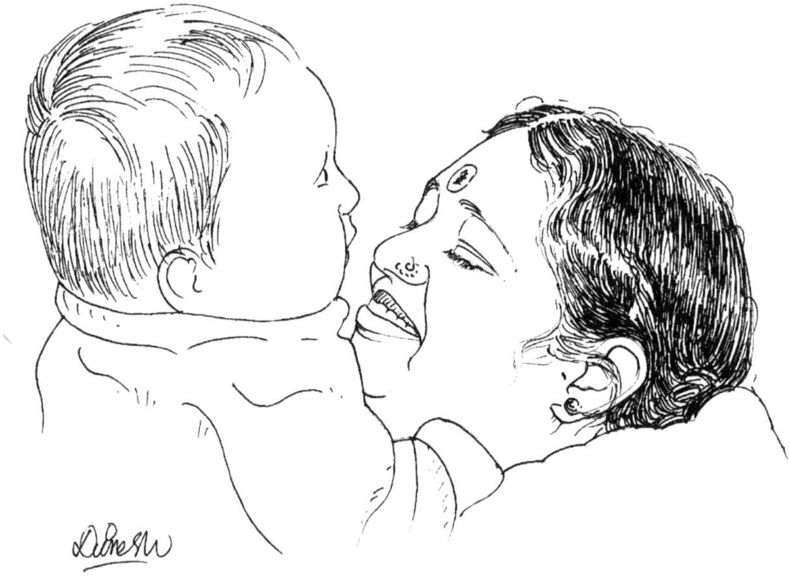

By Mother's Side Again

25

Although surrounded by material prosperity, people today wander here and there, not knowing what contentment is. Pure qualities are fast disappearing from human beings. In life's journey toward contentment, people are doomed to die like animals, unable to taste peace even once. What do human beings do that birds and beasts don't? The nests birds build are more beautiful than the splendid mansions human beings erect. Honeybees build their hives based on precise mathematical calculations at speeds that would astonish even expert engineers. Nature had already released its own aircraft long before people created airplanes! We modeled airplanes after birds and butterflies.

The ṛshis had already discovered everything in the inner Self, and had experienced the whole universe within themselves. Though omniscient, they lived as if ignorant of everything. As long as we dwell in the realm of duality, life may seem to be full of sorrows. What mahātmas like Amma give us is a training that enables us to see Oneness even in this world of polarities.

In the thick of Mumbai's fast-paced life, I met another one of Amma's sons who had had her darśan many times before. Dāmu, who worked at the Bhābha Research Center, used to come to Sāndīpani Sādhanālaya from time to time. He was a junior scientist and he used to attend *Bhagavad Gīta* classes and other satsangs regularly. During my stay in Mumbai, Dāmu's presence was a great consolation. I had many opportunities to open up my heart to talk about Amma. Dāmu never bothered to dress up or look good, ate only once daily, and led a life of utter renunciation. On moonlit nights, we used to walk along deserted lanes, talking about Amma. Often, we would be unaware of how long we had walked. There were days when we used to walk until dawn. We would then have to take a train back to the place from which we had set off.

Seven months had passed since I reached Mumbai. The more I appreciated Amma's greatness, the more difficult it became to stay away from her. I decided to quit my job and return to Vaḷḷickāvu. I wrote to Amma many times. Finally, she gave me permission to return. And so, I bid adieu to my life in Mumbai and returned home. Dāmu had to continue working in Mumbai for a much longer time. Eventually, he too became an āśram resident. Dāmu later became Swāmi Prajnānāmṛtānanda Puri.

A lot of changes had taken place in the āśram during those months I was away. Amma had accepted the name 'Mātā Amṛtānandamayi Devi' ['Divine Mother of Immortal Bliss'] that her children bestowed upon her. A trust known as 'Mātā Amṛtānandamayi Mission,' which included Amma's householder devotees, had been registered. This trust later became the Mātā Amṛtānandamayi Maṭh. In accordance with Amma's wish, I was appointed the Maṭh's General Secretary. A few new huts had sprung up near the one Amma was staying in. The first residents of the āśram did not have even one hut to stay in. Amma herself taught us how to braid the leaves of the coconut tree for building a hut and how to thatch a roof. I realized later that it was a part of the training to prepare us for doing everything without relying on others. When devotees came to the āśram, we had to vacate the huts for them. Devotees from various places used to come to the āśram on bhāva darśan days. After serving them food, there would be nothing left. Amma herself would go to the neighboring houses and bring back some food for us. In the refreshing coolness of Amma's love, āśram life became enchanting.

My family members had no objection to my resigning my job in Mumbai and returning. Amma used to send me to my pūrvāśram once a month. One day when I was there, my father noticed that the *muṇḍu*[24] I was wearing was patched in many places. He said that I should not wear a torn muṇḍu and gave me a new one. I returned to the āśram wearing the new one. While talking to Amma in her room, I did not notice the hem of my muṇḍu brushing against some lit incense sticks on the ground. When she saw my muṇḍu on fire, Amma beat out the flames with her bare hands. Noticing the new muṇḍu, she asked, "Son, where did you get this new muṇḍu?"

I explained to her what had happened when I had gone home.

"Son, don't you have another muṇḍu?" Hearing Amma's question, I shook my head to indicate a 'no.' Amma remained silent for some time. "Isn't everything that my all-renouncing children need supposed to reach here? My children need never go in search of anything. God will provide everything you need. Son, search your room thoroughly."

When I heard Amma's words, I recalled something. For many days, I had seen a paper-wrapped parcel in my room. I had thought some devotee had left it there and forgotten to take it back. I told Amma about the parcel. She told me to fetch it quickly. I came back with the parcel and passed it to her. She opened it. There were two new muṇḍus in there! Amma looked into my face. She said, "Didn't Amma tell you God will deliver whatever is necessary?"

[24] A cloth men tie around the waist, used for covering the lower half of the body.

The statements mahātmas make come true. Every word of Amma becomes a truth that can be experienced. All that we need tomorrow will arrive today itself. This was what the lessons that followed taught me. I have never needed to go in search of anything. Once we have surrendered our lives to God, we need never doubt. The thought that we are safe in her hands will infuse us with vigor and enthusiasm.

Amma is truly a flow of divine wisdom. No matter how much we may learn about her, she remains a vast ocean of knowledge. It may be that we may not understand Amma if we have seen her, gone near her, or stayed with her. As God lies beyond the ken of our intellects, the conclusions our minds draw are likely to be foolish. Arjuna lived with Śri Kṛshṇa for many years. He treated the Lord as a friend. Lord Kṛshṇa also went along with all of Arjuna's pranks. The Lord was not ready to impart divine wisdom to Arjuna at that time. However, when Arjuna was ready to surrender his ego totally during the Kurukshetra battle, the Lord unlocked His treasure chest of wisdom. When one realizes one's helplessness, the attitude of surrender will arise. The Guru causes our ego to wear away.

The patient may feel that the doctor cleaning the wound has no mercy. However, the doctor has no choice if he or she is to remove an infection that can spread throughout the body. When the shell of the ego is being cracked open, the disciple may feel some pain. The very disciple who had until then been singing the praises of the Guru may even insult the Guru. He may even leave the Guru and wallow in the world of *tamas* [inertia] yet again. Like the soul of the deceased that has not gained enough merit, it falls yet again under a hail of curses from nature and burns in hellfire.

It is out of compassion alone that God comes down into our midst in the form of the Guru. Amma has incarnated as the embodiment of sacrifice, ready to suffer and take upon herself the entire burden of the world's sins. Tormenting her own body and burning herself up, she is spreading the fragrance of love. For those who have inhaled that fragrance, God is no mere ideation, but a direct experience.

The Divine Bhāvas Within

26

During the Satya Yuga [Age of Truth], there was no need for temples. People had total faith in Gurus, who were enlightened. The hearts of people then were as immaculate as temple shrines. That is why they were able to behold and feel the resplendent Lord within all the time.

Those who lived with the conviction that divine strength was working within them did not come under the spell of the ego but attained oneness with the Paramātma.

Whenever divine incarnations enacted their līlās among human beings, there were many disbelievers. Few had total faith. No matter how many glories we may witness, if our minds are not pure, they can erect fences of doubt. No matter how much someone loves us, if we let ourselves listen often enough to someone else criticizing that person, our minds will start doubting. How can those with such fickle natures ever know God?

Our ṛshis had foreseen this. They realized that in the future, people would not find it easy to perceive the divine within or surrender completely to mahātmas. They infused their divine consciousness into idols. The temples that mahātmas thus consecrated became, in due course, hallowed places of worship.

It is said that the 33 crore deities exist within us all; everyone of us is heir to the infinite divine bhāvas. This human birth has been given to us so that we may nourish the divine virtues within and attain Fullness. In mahātmas, we can clearly behold all the attributes of God. The blessed ones who worship and seek refuge in mahātmas in order to find fulfillment in their lives can, in relatively few human years, be freed from the shackles of karma and the cycle of birth and death. Having gained the experience of bliss, they will attain immortality.

I am reminded of an incident that took place in the āśram many years ago. There was a festival being held in a temple near the āśram. As part of the rites, the idol in the temple would be brought out before the festival started, and taken on a procession to the houses in the village; the villagers believed that God was visiting their homes. The priest would carry on his head the idol in which the divinity had been invoked, and visit every house. The villagers would welcome the divinity with due devotion and reverence, ushering it into the house with a vessel filled with paddy, a lit oil lamp and other auspicious offerings of gifts. A group of ceremonial drummers accompanied the idol to the house next to the āśram. They did not enter the āśram. Devi Bhāva was going on then. Devotees sitting near Amma asked, "Amma, this is the only place they haven't visited. Can't you make them come here?"

Amma just smiled. After some time, the devotees noticed the sounds of the drums becoming louder and louder. It appeared as if the sounds were drawing nearer. Before long, the devotees witnessed an amazing spectacle. The man carrying the idol started moving in a trance-like dance, and rushed into the āśram. The drummers followed him, and the villagers ran after the drummers. After putting the idol on the ground, the priest returned to his senses. Immediately, he picked up the idol, put it on his head and started walking away. Everyone noticed Amma closing her eyes for some time.

After a short while, the priest again started dancing in abandon and ran into the āśram, lowering the idol there. When he regained his senses, he took the idol and walked away, just as he had done the last time. Amma once again closed her eyes. That man returned again, dancing in trance. This phenomenon recurred eight times. Finally, the man became utterly spent. He placed the idol in front of the kaḷari and appeared before Amma who was giving Devi Bhāva darśan. He extended his hand to get some *tīrtham* [consecrated water]. Amma gave him some tīrtham and, with great affection, drew him into her arms. After prostrating remorsefully before Amma, he picked up the idol and walked away.

The devotees stood watching all this, utterly amazed. Some could not understand what had just happened. How was it that whenever Amma closed her eyes, the priest would start his trance-like dance? Hearing their question, Amma smiled again. Everything is within Amma. The different aspects of divinity exist within us, but they are not under our control. However, all deities are subservient to knowers of the Truth, who can manifest or subdue any divine bhāva. For those who know that the 33 crore divine bhāvas exist within them, it is not difficult to rouse or contain these bhāvas. Devotees can see that during the Devi Bhāva, Amma manifests the divine bhāvas of Jagadambika, the Divine Mother of the Universe.

What we need to do is to get rid of the demonic tendencies within. In order to do so, we need to awaken positive qualities. When divine qualities grow, the divinity within us becomes more manifest. When demonic tendencies disappear, we gain sufficient purity to behold the entire pantheon of deities within. It is to gain this purity that we worship God.

It is said that the mind is like a key. If we turn it one way, we lock it. If we turn it the other way, we unlock it. Similarly, the mind can be the cause of our getting caught up in samsāra; conversely, we can use it to liberate ourselves from all bondage. The mind must be filled with noble thoughts. In order to do so, Amma reminds us to live with the remembrance of God, but most people put the power of imagination to wrong uses.

God is like the sun, which sheds light all the time. It imparts light and strength to all alike. Those who shut themselves up in darkness will not get sunlight. Likewise, God is constantly showering blessings upon us. The veils of the ego prevent divine grace from reaching us. In order to remove these veils, the Guru is necessary. This is what we can learn from Amma's life. There is no head that has not bowed down before her love. There is no heart that has not melted before her self-sacrifice. In the light of Amma's wisdom, the darkness created by the ego is dispelled. Deeds done without egoism become worship of the Lord.

There was once a thief who used to break into a coconut grove adjoining a house every night and steal coconuts. After the theft, he would throw a coconut into a sacrificial fire, and offer it prayerfully to Lord Gaṇapati as an act of atonement. He would then accept the cooked coconut as prasād from the Lord, eat it and leave. He would do this regularly. After some time, the thief became ill. As a result, he could no longer climb coconut trees. Nevertheless, every night, he would go to where he used to offer Lord Gaṇapati the coconut. He tried to console himself, thinking that the disease was punishment for stealing. Every day, he would pray to the Lord to forgive him for all his sins. His real sorrow lay in the fact that he was unable to offer the Lord anything. One midnight, Lord Gaṇapati appeared before the thief, who was languishing in the coconut grove. Within moments, he became freed of his disease. As proof of the Lord's appearance, a Gaṇesh statue manifested itself in that spot. Devotees built a temple there. Tens of thousands of coconuts came to be offered there. Innumerable people found solace there. That temple became a center through which thousands of people found fulfillment of their desires. Divine strength works in such a way that the innocent desire of even a thief becomes fulfilled.

God is ready to grant us anything when we surrender to Him. He does not come running to us after considering our history. When the eyes become wet in remembrance of the Lord, showers of blessings pour forth of their own accord.

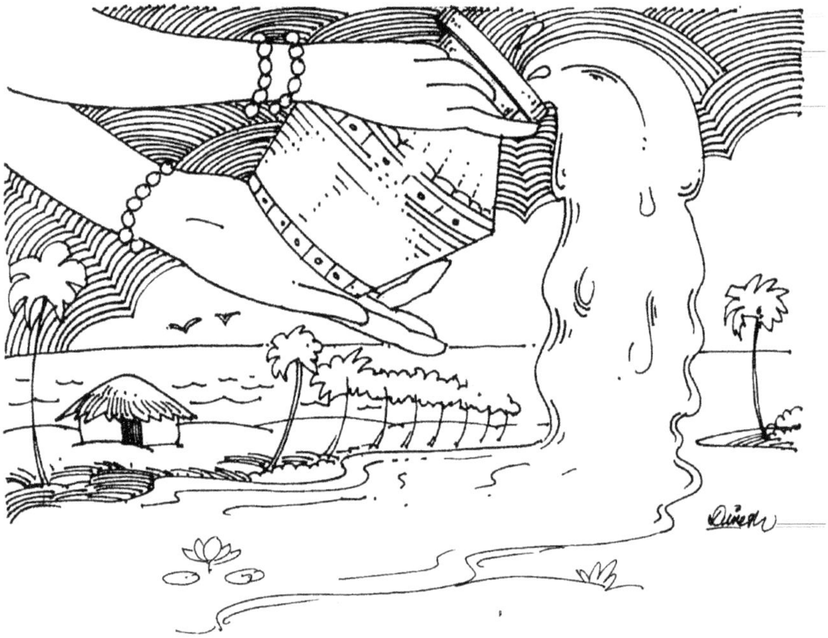

Annapūrṇeśvari

27

It is human nature to seek knowledge. Life is after all a journey toward Fullness, and the feeling that one is incomplete is the cause of suffering in worldly life. Since omniscience is the true nature of human beings, there is a longing in each one of us to know everything. We have an interest not only in our own affairs, but also in those of others and in the world too. We strive to learn about all these matters, but no intellectual striving can ever quench our thirst for knowledge. It is like Lord Gaṇesha's hunger—even after swallowing the whole universe, he remained hungry. However, his hunger became sated after he received just a handful of puffed rice from Parameśvara. Only a Satguru can quench the thirst for wisdom. To a disciple who had spent his whole life seeking the Truth, the Guru whispered into his ear, "Tat tvam asi"—O child, you are that very Truth!

The Guru's utterances take the disciple, who has devoured scholarly volumes, to the ineffable realms of experience. This, in turn, begets the dawn of wisdom.

Truth bestows true knowledge. Truth creates beauty in us. Truth is Śiva. 'Śiva' means 'the Imperishable.' All that is imperishable is splendid. In the luster of the radiant soul-consciousness, everything becomes resplendent. People usually turn to transient objects in search of happiness. We realize in hindsight that all transient objects are sources of sorrow. Those who strive during their lives to make transient objects their own will regret later. Therefore, embrace the Imperishable; gain soul beauty. Utilize the body and mind for this purpose. Death will snatch away all gains; therefore, strive to gain immortality. Transcend time. Seek refuge in Lord Yama, the Vanquisher of Time. Surrender yourself to the glorious Guru who has the power to burn away your sense of individuality in the fire of wisdom. This is the message of mahātmas.

An incident that happened years ago during Amma's birthday celebrations comes to mind. To inaugurate the birthday celebrations, a lamp had been lit on the veranda of the kaḷari, where Amma used to give bhāva darśans. After pada pūja to Amma, bhajans began. While the devotees were sitting, absorbed in the bhajans, a man started walking quickly through the mass of devotees toward Amma. Since Amma's eyes were closed, she did not appear to notice him. The devotees also seemed not to have noticed him. All eyes were riveted on Amma. As soon as the bhajan was over, the man whispered something into Amma's ear. It was clear from his facial expression that the matter was of some seriousness. Amma caressed the man and consoled him. No one understood what the matter was. When bhajans were over, Amma distributed prasād to all the devotees, and then walked toward the kitchen. Some of us followed Amma. When we reached the kitchen, we realized what had happened. The cook was missing! Although 3,000 devotees had come to the āśram that day, a traditional feast had been prepared for only 500 people. No one had expected that so many devotees would come!

The food had been prepared based on the number of people present in the āśram that morning. Provisions had not been arranged for more people either. The cook, seeing no way out of the predicament, had probably fled the scene. Amma consoled the desperate people in the kitchen, and took upon herself the task of serving the food.

The devotees sat down in rows in the thatched shed built next to the structure where Vedanta classes were conducted. People living in the nearby coastal areas had arrived with vessels to take food back to their homes. This is how it is in villages; if there is a feast in some place, food will be sent to the houses of those who cannot attend. Amma started serving. When they saw how she was serving, those in the kitchen became alarmed. We had thought that Amma would serve less so that everyone would get food. However, she confounded our expectation, and served heaped ladles instead. How was one to tell her to serve less? Even if we had, she would not have obeyed. She has never been known for her obedience, even in the past! *Trikāla jñānis* [enlightened ones who know everything about the past, present and future] do not need anyone's advice. Nevertheless, some of us have tried to advise her occasionally.

I have told Amma many times, "God too needs to be obedient occasionally!" I had reasons for saying so. If told to rest, she will not rest. If told to eat, she will not eat. When it is time to sleep, she will not sleep. Seeing her sacrificing her body like this all the time, I often wished that Amma would be as obedient as the gods in the temple. In a temple, one can offer consecrated food to the deity. One can put Him to sleep. At night, the priest can lock up the temple and return home. One cannot do that here. The reason is, the God here does not even enter the house! She sits on the ground in front of the kaḷari and meditates. She gives darśan there in that very place. A small hut had been constructed for Amma. A two-story building had also been completed with the plan to use the room below as a meditation room, and the room above as Amma's room. But if Amma preferred to lie on the ground, what could we do? As a result, we too had the good fortune of learning how nice it was to sleep outside on the bare ground.

During my childhood, I yearned to get wet in the rain, but my parents would not allow me; I would catch a fever, they said. I suppose they were right; those unused to getting wet in the rain will fall sick. Forest dwellers living in the open, exposed to both the sunlight and rain, never get a fever. I have seen Amma dancing in bliss in lashing downpours. The pleasure of getting drenched by rain can only be known through experience, right? I have never since felt like staying in during any storm. I used to wait for every opportunity to step out into heavy rains to receive nature's *abhishekam* [ceremonial bath]. Amma taught us to relish extreme heat, heavy rains and intense cold.

Seeing the way in which Amma was serving food, some of the alarmed householder devotees suggested, "Dearest Amma, what about serving a little less?"

Amma paid no heed to what they said. One of the grandfathers from the village muttered, "There's no point in telling her anything! She has always had the habit of giving generously."

Amma continued serving. The food vessels were emptying out. Amma was serving rapidly.

"If Little One serves, no one will be left wanting," Damayanti-amma (Amma's mother) asserted resolutely; so firm was her faith. How many wondrous līlās Damayanti-amma, who has had the singular fortune of being Amma's mother, has seen! When they heard those words, those who had been watching Amma serve, with bated breath, felt relieved and reassured. Amma finished ladling food into the last banana leaf. Wonder of wonders—even after serving more than 3,000 people, there was still rice and curries left in the food vessels! To those of us who were gazing wonderstruck at Amma's face, she responded with a sweet smile.

"Children, can love be measured and quantified? Love can never be exhausted. Anything that runs out cannot be love either. It is the love of the children here who worked hard that filled the food vessels."

Amma always takes pains to point out that everything is due to the power of her children's love, and never her own divine might. God, after all, loves to glorify His devotee. He never has the feeling of doing anything. He is egoless. How can someone who has become transformed into pure love itself have an ego?

What isn't possible for one who has become the embodiment of love? A long time ago, many people from Ālappāḍ had witnessed the sight of Amma serving *pancāmṛtam* (sweet pudding made from five ingredients) from a tiny vessel to a thousand people. It seems that even after everyone had been served, the tiny vessel was still brimming with pancāmṛtam! On that day, it was Amma's love itself that had overflowed as pancāmṛtam.

"If Amma continues showering so much love, won't it run out in the end?" A devotee raised this doubt.

Amma gave a clear answer. "Never! Children, it will never run out. I only dispense what overflows. It's not something I consciously set out to do. Love just overflows."

If the love that overflows from Amma is so vast, how can one measure the oceanic love that fills her heart?

It is said that when Durvāsa and his vast retinue vicariously ate Pāncāli's love-filled spinach piece, they felt full[25]! We have also heard

[25] Pāncāli and the Pāṇḍavas had been blessed with an akshaya pātram, a food vessel that auto-replenishes itself. That day, after the Pāṇḍavas had eaten their mid-day meal, Pāncāli had hers, and then washed the vessel... ... When she learned that Sage Durvāsa and his retinue of thousands were coming to her hermitage for lunch, she became anxious, because the sage was known for his fiery temper and for cursing those who incurred his wrath. She prayed fervently to Lord Kṛshṇa who appeared before her and asked her for something to eat. Pāncāli replied that, as she had already washed the akshaya pātram, there was

the story of how Christ fed 5,000 people with five loaves of bread and two fishes. But have we seen all this for ourselves? Rationalists among us may, therefore, dismiss these stories as apocryphal.

However, the stories of Amma's incarnation did not take place centuries ago. It is the experience of many thousands who are still alive today. Lord Kṛshṇa showed the world what great wonders love can create. If we can imbibe that same love through a mother's affection, everything will appear wondrous to us.

Amma has said that the world is supported by love. In order to become the embodiments of pure love, we must dive into the ocean of love that is Amma. This is real surrender. Self surrender takes us to a state in which we yearn to embrace Truth.

* * *

Mahātmas don't perform miracles, but everything they do becomes a miracle. It's not that mahātmas speak the truth; everything they say comes true! When people who come for Amma's darśan pray for their troubles to be removed and their desires to be fulfilled, she says, "Amma will make a sankalpa."

What does it mean? The sankalpas of jñānis are never made in vain. These sankalpas generate powerful vibrations in nature, which will start facilitating the fulfillment of the sankalpas at once.

When I was staying with Amma in the āśram, it was my duty to translate English letters into Malayāḷam and read them aloud to her, and to write down her reply to those who had sent these letters. I've seen Amma carefully reading the thousands of letters sent to her, no matter how much time it may take. If someone

---

nothing left. Kṛshṇa asked her to check the vessel again. Pāncāli saw a tiny piece of spinach and humbly offered the piece to the Lord, who ate and proclaimed Himself sated. Durvāsa and his retinue, who were bathing in a river, felt sated too, and thus decided to forgo lunch that day.

hides the letters so that she can rest, Amma will hunt them out and read all of them.

One day, when Amma had returned to her room after the morning darśan, I went there as usual with the letters. I read each of the letters to her. Since there were many letters, I had to read them quickly. In those days, Amma would lie down on the bare ground and listen to the letters being read. All my attention was focused on the letters, which I was reading aloud without stopping. Suddenly, I heard a sound behind me. *Boom!* I turned around. Amma had rolled on the ground like a child and was behind me!

Amma told me, "Son, that 'boom' was the sound of the cat falling into the pond. Nothing to worry about. It knows how to swim!"

It was only then that I realized Amma had been lying there, reading a comic book! I didn't like it one bit. Chagrined, I said, "Here I am, taking the trouble to translate the letters. If this is how it's going to be, I'm going to stop reading them!"

"Don't get angry, darling. A child gave me this book during the morning darśan. He gave it to me with so much love and said that I should read it after darśan. I could not ignore his innocent sankalpa. Son, Amma was also paying attention to what you were reading."

I wasn't prepared to listen to anything she had to say. I asked her to tell me what the contents of the letters I had read out to her were. Amma related the contents of the 10 odd letters I had read out to her.

She then said, "Now, son, listen also to what the unopened letters say."

She then told me the contents of every single one of those unopened letters! She had understood the contents of all of them even before they had been opened. When I opened the letters, I realized that everything she said had been totally correct.

Amazed, I asked her, "Amma, you know the contents of all these letters even without reading them. Why then do you make me spend so much time translating them for you to hear?"

Amma replied, "Even the poor, who lack the means to post a letter, send letters to Amma through others. When these people write letters, they do so with the sankalpa that Amma should read them. Amma can't help but bow down to their heartfelt sankalpas."

She continued, "At the time the innocent children write the letters, their sankalpas are already recorded in nature. Through the loving letters of their hearts, their messages reach Amma faster than the posted letters."

It's not through letters that the mother knows the hunger of her child, is it? In the deep bond of love between mother and child, their hearts become one. Similarly, mahātmas who are one with the universe in their love can feel the thought vibrations of all creatures in themselves.

The Blunders of a Disciple

28

It is said that two things in the world are unending: the Guru's compassion and the disciple's stupidity. Memories of my follies during the early days with Amma come to mind from time to time. This was the time I had just started staying in the āśram. Amma would spend all her time with us. Just as a mother hen would carefully watch over its brood of chicks, we had ample opportunities to bask under Amma's protective wings. In those days, it was impossible for us to stay away from her for even a moment; such was the state of our minds then. We would meditate together, sing bhajans together and dance together. From time to time, Amma would play some pranks and make us roar with laughter. Even in those days, when one could forget everything in the intoxication of devotion brought on by the Satguru's presence, I made some blunders.

The notions of spirituality I had before joining the āśram were markedly different. I imagined I would never again have to return to material life. I thought Amma would let us undergo austerities in the Himālayan peaks or in the heart of some forest in order to attain God. She kept changing my false ideas about spirituality.

I decided to do my spiritual practices with utmost seriousness in order to get closer to Amma. I also determined upon the means to behold Amma's real form and to get closer to her—learn Devi Pūja. Someone told me that if one worshipped Devi without any lapse, one could become closer to Amma and have the divine vision of Devi. Accordingly, I attempted to learn Devi Pūja. From the devotee who had advised me to learn the pūja, I obtained both the utensils needed for doing the pūja and an idol of Devi.

I thus became engaged in doing pūja. Amma noticed that I would spend a long time polishing the pūja vessels until they shone. I thought that if one did pūja with vessels that glittered like gold, Devi would be easily pleased. Therefore, I would spend more time than was necessary in polishing the pūja vessels.

One morning, while doing pūja in my hut, Amma came in. I had thought Amma would give me darśan in the form of Devi, but she appeared in her usual form. I felt proud of the power of my pūja. How quickly I had managed to summon Amma with my efforts! The illusion that Amma had come because she was pleased with my pūja didn't last too long though. In fact, you could say all my calculations went awry. There wasn't even an iota of joy in Amma's expression; instead, her face wore a grave look. "Son, there's no need to do pūja anymore," she said. "It's enough if you do *mānasa pūja*."

When I heard her words, I was petrified. Even before I could ask anything, Amma picked up all my pūja vessels and left. In this way, my pūja sādhana came to an end.

I later thought that one could make spiritual progress through scriptural study. At this time, Amma engaged a Sanskṛt scholar to teach us the language. The study of Sanskṛt soon became an all-consuming passion. I began to miss many of my daily spiritual practices, spending all my time studying Sanskṛt. Amma was observing all this. I imagined that if she learned that I was earnestly studying the scriptures, she would love me more. Instead, something else happened.

One night at two o'clock, while studying Sanskṛt grammar under lantern light, Amma suddenly entered the hut. She saw that instead of meditating as I used to at that time, I was boning up on grammar. I wasn't even aware that Amma was there, so engrossed was I in memorizing grammar rules! She gathered all my Sanskṛt texts and walked out. I thus decided to temporarily stop my Sanskṛt studies too.

I realized that Amma did not like it that I was skipping my daily spiritual practices. If that was the case, she would presumably like it if I did intense spiritual practices. There was no other choice—I had to practice the severest austerities that would elevate me to the peaks of spirituality! It wasn't difficult to obtain Amma's permission. She agreed to let me perform tapas in the cave.

"Son, how long do you intend to stay there?" Amma asked.

Unable to give an answer immediately, I kept quiet. Later on, I said, "Forty-one days."

Amma smiled and gave me permission to practice tapas. However, I did not understand the meaning of the smile then. The next day, I got up early in the morning and entered the cave. I commenced my practices. After some time, the sounds of Amma's boisterous laugh from in front of the kaḷari reached my ears. When I heard that laughter, I was unable to sit still for much longer. I got up and peeped through the door. My brothers Bālu, Veṇu and Rao were sitting around Amma, who was cracking jokes and making them laugh. I could not clearly hear what Amma was saying. Slowly, I walked away from the cave and sat down behind Amma. Hearing my footsteps, Amma turned around. When she saw me, Amma laughed and asked, "Dear Śri, when are you going to start your tapas in the cave?"

I had not told her that I was going to start my tapas early that morning. The truth was that my mind was already suffering badly from the pangs of separation from Amma. She looked at me compassionately, as if to encourage me. I hung my head so that she would not see the tears welling up in my eyes.

When I had informed Amma about my desire to perform tapas, I had not thought about how painful it would be to stay away from her physically. The next day, I entered the cave again and started my austerities. A few hours must have passed when I heard the sounds of bhajans outside. My mind moved toward the sounds. No matter how hard I tried to control myself, it proved impossible for me to continue sitting there. Although I told myself that I would not even get up, I could not help doing so! Standing at the entrance to the cave, I looked outside. Amma was singing bhajans with the brahmacāris. Many devotees from Kollam were sitting all around. In those days, I was the one who used to play the harmonium for Amma. I peered closely to see who was playing the harmonium for her now. It was Nealu. I dashed out of the cave! Amma told all those around her what had really happened. They all looked at me and started laughing. I stood there helplessly, feeling utterly miserable. Without saying a word, I walked back to the cave, got in and sat down. I vowed this would never happen again.

I had to honor the word I had given Amma. I resolved not to step out of the cave until the 41 days were over. The first few days were very difficult. Whenever I heard Amma's voice, the longing to see her would threaten to break all vows. I prayed to Amma herself to give me the strength to overcome this difficulty. If only Amma would come into the cave, I thought wistfully. Thinking that she would come, I remained awake at night, waiting for her. But she never came. I began to reconcile myself to the environment of the cave.

One day, Amma entered the cave. Her love and affection infused new life into me. "Son, when you emerge from the cave, you must bring Devi-amma with you," she reminded me.

I later realized that she had blessed me to have the experience of the Goddess [Devi] that is Amma dwelling in the heart. In the days that followed, I truly experienced the constant proximity to Amma even though she was physically distant. If not for this experience, I would not have been able to continue in that cave. Thus I spent my time there, meditating on Amma.

One day, I heard Amma's voice yet again from in front of the cave. "Śri-mon, 41 days have passed. Aren't you coming out?"

I was unable to reply. My mind had reconciled itself totally to the cave environment. Two days later, Amma came into the cave and dragged me out. Bursting into laughter, she said, "Son, one who remembers the Guru incessantly is doing tapas whether he is inside the cave or outside. That being the case, there is no need to do tapas in the cave. Once an inner bond with the Guru has been forged, all actions will become an austerity."

I have read that the Guru's physical presence is unquestionably necessary in the initial stages of a disciple's sādhana. If we can live with an attitude of surrender in the Guru's presence, there is nothing we will not be able to accomplish. I realized that trying to stay away from Amma's physical presence, at a time when she used to spend 24 hours a day dancing and singing with her children, had been foolish. I had lost 41 invaluable golden days. Amma consoled me with kind words of blessings.

What is of utmost importance is incessant remembrance of the Guru. We should try to make as much use as possible of the Guru's presence. An opportunity to be in the presence of mahātmas is a rare blessing. It is difficult enough to come by a human birth. Even more difficult is having an interest in matters spiritual. The most difficult thing to gain is proximity to a mahātma. This is what we get from Amma's presence. We should obey Amma's words with loving faith and devotion. Instead of trying to quell our likes and dislikes on our own, we should let Amma guide us.

We need to develop the strength to get the better of unfavorable circumstances, and learn to think beyond our likes and dislikes. Cultivating expansiveness of mind and heart will enable us to feel compassion for the sorrows of the world. We must become aware of our selfishness and bad habits, and eliminate them. We should try to get rid of our egos. These are all part of spiritual life. Amma has created the external circumstances for achieving these ends. That is why, in the Guru's presence, we can achieve within a very short time what would otherwise have required many ages of tapas to accomplish. Amma's every movement imparts more wisdom than thousands of books. If we can understand the myriad expressions that flash on her face every moment, if we can understand the import of the changing mudras her fingers display, it is unlikely that we will need anything else for gaining spiritual wisdom.

Spirituality is not just about performing pūjas, studying Sanskṛt or the scriptures, or immuring oneself in a cave; it is an outlook that lends one strength to face all kinds of situations. It is the beauty of the bliss-bestowing dissociation that makes life an art. Our every move should become a spiritual practice. Spiritual science is the wisdom that enables one to make life splendid by spreading the fragrance and beauty of love without letting the world taint us, just like the lotus that grows in mud.

At present, everything we do with our minds or bodies is sheer folly. It will never end unless we transcend the mind. We may amass a large amount of information. We can become a veritable treasury of encyclopedic knowledge. Nevertheless, we will continue re-enacting our inanities time and again. To quote Amma's words, "We have knowledge, but no awareness." Amma is transmitting the wisdom that will lead us to the highest awareness.

Our lives should be wholly dedicated to spiritual practice. Countless devotees, Amma's children, who have made the work they do a spiritual practice and have thus become worthy of God's blessings, are now doing selfless service in various parts of the world. Amma is encouraging them to gain inner purity through selfless service. Not everyone may be able to take the same path to God-realization. Top-grade aspirants, those rich in satvic qualities, are rare. Most express predominantly rajasic or tamasic qualities in their habits. That is why the Guru prescribes a spiritual path suited to the disciple's mental constitution.

Most people pay heed only to their own affairs throughout their lives. What makes us deserving of God's blessings is selfless work. Even if we are working for our near and dear ones, we should try to do so with a selfless attitude. Selfless deeds will fill our lives with beauty and contentment.

Cosmic delusion, fraught with dualities, is the cause of all suffering. We see what we should not, and we do not see what we ought to! In order to see the world as it really is, we need inner purity. If the eyes of wisdom are to open, we need the Guru's grace, for it is only through her grace that the vision of Truth can displace our world-oriented consciousness. Shedding our karmic burdens, our lives in this world should become a pilgrimage toward Wholeness. This samsāra is only as good as an apprenticeship. We should capitalize on this divine life in order to become a *paramahamsa* [exalted saint], a state that transcends all dualities. The Guru's presence is where we can do so.

The love that overflows from our hearts should manifest as *seva*, but we should first learn to serve the Guru. Who cannot love a Satguru like Amma, who brims with divine qualities? How enthusiastic everyone is to serve her holy feet! In the early days of the āśram, everyone would compete to serve Amma. The problems that this competition among devotees yielded were not few. I now realize that I, too, was one among those devotees.

A part of the hut where Amma rested was used as a kitchen. Usually, Swāmi Rāmakṛshṇānanda would make morning tea for her. One day, when he was not in the āśram, I decided to make tea for her. I had never before in my life made tea. Yet I bustled about as though I ran a teashop! It is the disciple's duty to serve the Guru, isn't it? How could I waste this opportunity to serve Amma? Even before anyone else could get a chance to step into the kitchen, I announced my intention to make tea for Amma. Not only that, I even told Amma in advance about my intention. Therefore, no one came to bother me.

After half an hour, Amma called out from in front of the kaḷari, "Śri-mon, where's the tea?"

"I'm making it," I loudly called out in reply.

Amma personally came to the kitchen to see how I was preparing my special tea. Seeing the color of the water boiling in the vessel, Amma asked, "Son, why is it so black?"

"I was also wondering about it, Amma. I've made several attempts now, but I still can't figure out why the water is so black!"

Without paying attention to what I was saying, Amma picked up the teapot. "There is something wrong with this tea powder. No matter how many times I try, Amma, it's not coming out right." I confessed my helplessness. I opened the tin containing the tea powder and showed it to Amma. When she saw it, she started laughing loudly. How could the sight of tea elicit so much laughter? Not understanding what the matter was, I stood helpless. After some time, I realized what had happened. What I had put into hot water, considering it to be tea powder, had in fact been the burnt husk of paddy, used as teeth-cleaning powder! Amma gamely agreed that the mistake had been inadvertently caused by my confusing the teeth-cleaning powder for tea powder.

I said, "Amma, please don't tell anyone about this. Anyone can make mistakes. Why don't you go and sit in front of the kaḷari? I will finish preparing the tea in a few minutes and bring it to you!"

Like an obedient child, Amma went to sit on the kaḷari's open veranda and waited. Like an expert cook, I whipped up a cup of tea in no time at all. It didn't escape my notice that what I had pulled off was no small task. I walked proudly toward Amma with the tea. After taking a sip, Amma put the cup down on the ground and started rolling around on the floor, laughing. I had seen Amma doing this on various occasions when she went into samādhi. However, it had happened only during bhajans. I could not understand how a cup of tea could affect her like this. Perhaps I had chanted my mantra too many times while making tea! Anyway, I took a sip from the cup to see if I too would have the same experience. I then clearly understood the reason behind Amma's laughter. The fact that sugar and salt were of the same color and shape could, I realized, be such a dangerous thing; instead of adding sugar, I had added salt! Instead of serving Amma, I had troubled her! The truth pained me. In the end, Amma herself went into the kitchen, prepared tea and gave me a cup too. In Amma's face, which was overflowing with the sweetness of motherliness, there was nothing other than affection. The mesmerizing power of that divine love, which dispels the disciple's ignorance and ego, brought tears to my eyes.

The majority are those who, in serving the Guru, inconvenience her. We should do what we know and not insist on doing a seva someone else is doing.

The first *sevaks* who came to serve Amma were birds and beasts. Amma once said, "The birds and beasts were able to understand Amma immediately, but it has been difficult for human beings to understand her."

Often, innocence can fathom what the intellect cannot. All creatures came to understand the greatness of Amma, who had become one with nature. Human beings were the last to understand her. When Amma was not eating, eagles, cows and dogs would run to her to serve her, whereas human beings did not hesitate to call her crazy and mock her. Through their lives, birds and beasts can teach us many lessons. That is why the avadhūtas strove to see them as Gurus (*Avadhūta Gīta*). The so-called educated moderns often forget that the beings we consider unintelligent engage in selfless service. We do not learn any lesson from these mute creatures, and instead kill them for food. How can human beings get any peace in a world chock-a-block with the pain and distress of mute creatures wailing in slaughterhouses?

On many occasions, human beings have had to look on in numb shock as natural calamities, in a wild dance of destruction, toppled all that they erected. Yet, their lack of reverence for nature has not ceased. Great spiritual masters are being criticized, even today. Mahātmas who do only good are still being persecuted. Nevertheless, Amma continues to travel throughout the world, like an unstoppable flow from a perennial spring of love, praying for the welfare of those who criticize and mock her, and showering compassion on all.

Marvels of Divine Love

29

I recall how every passing day presented us with an abundance of experiences. Amma was creating around her a microcosm of the world, with touching scenes that strung together children of different inclinations on the thread of her love, transforming them into a garland for the Lord, an adornment for the world. Amma's presence—which transforms an idol into a deity, renders all defects beautiful, and melts the ego—has turned the spiritual world into the biggest university. She shines as the personification of self-sacrifice, providing innumerable opportunities for seekers to drink the nectar of divine love and dissolve in eternity, no matter how diverse their paths to the Truth. Successions of experiences that make us laugh and ponder occur daily around Amma.

In the early days of the āśram, there were no buildings. A few huts and the kaḷari where Amma used to give darśan—that was the āśram. Spiritual practices like japa and meditation were carried out on the banks of the backwaters. Most of the time, Amma would be on the ground in front of the kaḷari. She never used even a mat for lying down. Used to seeing her example of sacrifice, the āśram residents did the same. Brahmacāris used to vacate their huts for devotees visiting the āśram. There were many days when we had to go without food after cooking and serving the devotees. Often, when we lay on the bare ground without eating, after serving devotees food to their satisfaction, Amma would try to wake us up to make us eat. No matter how many days we went hungry, we never felt tired. Those were the days when we realized that happiness and satisfaction lay in sacrificing, not in taking. They were all filled with truly auspicious moments in our lives.

A devotee who stayed in the hut of Uṇṇikṛshṇan (now Swāmi Turīyāmṛtānanda Puri), who did pūja in the kaḷari, came back the next time with a new straw mat. He had felt sorry seeing Uṇṇi sleeping on the bare ground. He left after instructing Uṇṇi to henceforth lie down on the mat.

Another incident took place thereafter. A man from Kāṭṭūr happened to hear the bhajans that Amma's brahmacāris were singing in the Occira temple. An attraction to the bhajans led him to Amma. When he saw the unbelievable in Vaḷḷickāvu, he was astonished. He gazed with curiosity at the brahmacāris, who had, even at the onset of youth, become ready to sacrifice everything for the welfare of the world, and who were immersed in meditation along the banks of the backwaters. He gazed reverentially at those who had sought refuge at Amma's lotus feet, having abandoned all comforts in this modern age when people were running pell-mell after sensual pleasures. These āśram residents would sing hymns of devotion throughout darśan. They would work in the kitchen, cowshed and construction sites with an attitude of renunciation. He kept trying to find out more about these blessed brahmacāris of Amma. He spoke to each one of us personally. He even advised us to repeat the last line at the close of the bhajans three times.

Uṇṇi, who had composed the most number of bhajans, became the focal point of his attention. How did Uṇṇi compose so many beautiful poems? How could he compose songs that contained such abstruse spiritual principles without the benefit of instruction in Sanskṛt or higher education? If one has the Guru's grace, what isn't possible? He persistently tried to discover the secret behind Uṇṇi's poetry. He questioned brahmacāris and devotees closely. The clearest answer came from a devotee named Ayyappan who spent all his time reading in the coconut grove. Using wit to make one laugh is a good deed, isn't it? What transpired later was an example of this.

In a trice, Ayyappan concocted a story about the secret behind Uṇṇi's poetry, which he related to the Kāṭṭūr devotee. "Some years ago, a great yogi came here. He stayed for a few days and then left. Possessed of great occult powers, the yogi stayed in Uṇṇi's hut. He bequeathed to Uṇṇi the mat on which he used to lie down, one that was imbued with divine energy. The miracle took place after the yogi left. When Uṇṇi sat down on the mat, poems started welling up within. He started writing without stopping. From that day onward, Uṇṇi would sit on that mat whenever he wrote poetry!"

The devotee realized that the divine power of the straw mat was the secret behind Uṇṇi's poetry. That night, he stayed in the aśram.

When Uṇṇi woke up the next day and started rolling up his mat, he noticed that half his mat was missing! How had that happened? Uṇṇi showed everyone the remains of his mat. Everyone laughed, seeing the pitiable condition of the mat. However, no one knew why. Anyway, Uṇṇi was glad that he had lost half his mat. He did not have to use it anymore!

About two years later, Amma had programs in Kāṭṭūr, where she stayed in the house of that devotee. She opened the door to the pūja room and stepped inside. Everyone noticed a bundle wrapped in silk cloth and placed in front of the oil lamp. After doing the pūja, Amma asked the head of the household, "Son, what is in this bundle?"

Full of humility, the man replied, "Amma, why don't you open it up?"

Amma started removing the wrapping slowly. Everyone looked on in great anticipation. What could it be that he had placed so carefully before the oil lamp? One by one, Amma removed the many layers of glittering silk that had been used to wrap the bundle. Finally, seeing a piece of a tattered straw mat inside all the silk cloths, we burst into laughter. It was the piece of Uṇṇi's mat that had gone missing! Even those who didn't know the story behind it were laughing; those of us who knew the story couldn't control our laughter at all! Amma drew that innocent man into her arms and hugged him. After the incident, the man came to the āśram with poems he had composed. By Amma's grace, those poems were proof of the marvels innocent faith can create.

There is no end to the wonders that take place in Amma's sacred presence. For those jaded by boredom, there were the quaint thatched huts on the grounds in front of the kaḷari to evoke in them the enthusiasm and purity of a child. How many expressions of striving has the kaḷari been witness to! What everyone—devotee, scholar, rationalist, scientist, politician and religious leader—can gain from this blessed sanctuary is the divine experience of becoming one with a pure heart and a humble head.

From the stories of Kāḷidās's life, we know how Kāḷi's shower of compassion transformed a simpleton into a poet. In response to Kāḷi's question "Who's inside?" he did not say "Me." What he said was "Your servant." Can God desist from blessing someone with the attitude of a servant? Indeed, Mother Kāḷi showered him profusely with Her blessings.

Wonders continuously take place in this sacred abode too. The Satguru can make anyone an orator, scholar, bard or exalted devotee. If we are a tool in God's hands, we can become anything. A tool has no likes or dislikes, no complaints. A musical instrument patiently awaits the touch of the musician's fingers. It submits silently to the musician. All those who wait patiently for the Guru's shower of compassion, the way a bud performs austerities in order to blossom, can become unfading flowers that exude the sweet fragrance of spirituality.

* * *

There are stories also of how some, having realized that they can gain anything if they have Amma's blessings, strove to use her to get rid of their enemies. Many pay for pūjas that are aimed at destroying enemies to be performed in temples. However, what Devi destroys is not one's enemies but one's enmity. In other words, getting rid of enemies is the transforming of foes into friends.

One Tuesday night, while Devi Bhāva darśan was going on, a man walked into the kaḷari. Everyone noticed him as he chanted mantras loudly and entered the shrine, without heeding the long lines of people queuing up for darśan. As soon as he entered the kaḷari, he started showering Amma's head with flowers while intoning mantras. Amma closed her eyes and became immersed in meditation. She remained still for almost 10 minutes. When the man had finished offering the flowers, she opened her eyes. With a grave expression on her face, Amma asked him, "Son, is all that you do to the idol done to the body too?"

No one understood the meaning of Amma's question. "Amma, there was no other way. Please forgive me!"

Although those near the man heard his reply, they didn't understood what he was talking about.

"Now, it is enough if you just give me some flowers with your right hand, Amma. I will then leave immediately."

Amma took some flowers in her left hand and extended it. The man did not want to accept them. He insisted that Amma offer the flowers with her right hand, but Amma showed no sign of relenting. Those who were waiting for darśan became impatient. Finally, the man took some flowers and, pressing them on Amma's right hand, left with the flowers.

What had that man been doing? The devotees' anxiety increased. Amma merely smiled. For her, these were all līlās. The devotees who became entranced by the sweet smile of the mother who enjoys her children's mischief even forgot the question, but I didn't.

The next day, Amma herself explained what had happened. The man who had come chanting the mantras was the proprietor of a bakery. Amma clearly recalled having seen him come for darśan on many occasions. Another man had opened a shop next to his bakery, and this had caused a significant loss in the baker's revenue. He wanted to get rid of that shop at all costs. For this reason, he had supplicated Amma on numerous occasions. The belief that only the elimination of that shop owner would conduce to his own good had prompted him to seek Amma's help. When he realized that Amma would not be an accomplice to anything that would harm anyone, he approached a practitioner of black magic as a last resort. He learned some mantras that would force Devi to accomplish certain ends of his. It was while uttering those incantations that he showered Amma with flowers. It seems the sorcerer had told him that if Amma gave him flowers with her right hand, his plan would succeed!

"So, will things turn out as he intends?" I asked.

"No, son. Amma has made a sankalpa for his bakery to prosper. At the same time, Amma has done nothing that will cause the other man's shop to founder. That's why, when the man started offering flowers to the body while chanting mantras, Amma had to vacate the body for a short while." I recalled how Amma had remained utterly motionless, her eyes closed.

"He could offer flowers only to the inert body. Therefore, his intentions are not going to bear fruit. However, Amma is praying for his growth."

What isn't possible for mahātmas who can leave their bodies at will? They desire only good for the world. They cannot harm anyone. Their lives are lyrics of imperishable love. For as long as this world exists, the echo of that mantra of love will resound throughout the universe.

* * *

In life, the highest states of bliss can never be expressed by words. So many things that are beyond words happen all the time in Amma's sacred presence. All that we think is impossible can be achieved through innocent faith. What is needed is a heart that is pure enough to believe. We will then see all that transpires in the inner realms of consciousness becoming a reality.

The mind keeps vacillating all the time. It raises doubts. It seeks proof for the intellect. Just as leaves sprout on a tree, questions that breed doubts keep cropping up. Time is wasted in trying to find answers. What can be gained quickly through an attitude of surrender gets lost as a result of the mind's interference. The heart that overflows with love cannot doubt; it can only believe. It cannot even be said that it believes. Doubt is the child of fear, and faith, of love. Faith is only for those who can love, for where there is love, there is neither doubt nor complaint. Devotion is the fragrance of faith. Logic is the creation of a community that perishes without any sense of direction; it is not practical in life. A rationalist rushing his dying child to the hospital has blind faith in the doctor. He does not allow the doctor to treat his child only after he examines the doctor's license. He does not administer medicines to his child only after studying the chemical constituents of the medicine. This, too, is blind faith. The subtle, wayward tendencies of the mind encourage us to deny God. But when the ego's head has been lopped off, we become humble. In the presence of a Satguru like Amma, a child gains purity of mind and is able to recover its natural innocence. All faith is blind. Nevertheless, the faith that arises from surrender removes the darkness of ignorance. Love's divine effulgence dispels the shadows cast by doubt. This is what happens in the Guru's presence.

One day, while giving darśan, Amma asked a boy who was seated amid the devotees to come to her. She asked him to sit down next to her, and they spoke for a long time. His joy at having been recognized by Amma was evident on his face.

"Amma, you didn't forget me!" he said.

Hearing his words, Amma laughed. "Son, forgetting is hard, isn't it?"

I realized that her reply was not meant just for him. She was probably alluding to how difficult it was to reach a state in which one has forgotten everything else (but God).

That boy had first had the good fortune of having Amma's darśan a few months before, when devotees near Konni, in east Kerala, had accorded her a reception. After the program, there had been a house visit. As the devotees sang bhajans rapturously with Amma, she noticed a boy gazing at her devoutly. The man of the house introduced him to Amma. "Amma, he sings really well!" Amma drew him to her and blessed him. He sang a hymn in praise of Lord Ayyappa, which Amma enjoyed immensely.

That day, he was coming to the āśram for the first time to see Amma. He thought she wouldn't remember him, but from her words, he realized that she remembered even the lyrics of the song he had sung then. He continued sitting next to Amma until darśan ended. He wanted to tell Amma something, but was unable to bring himself to do so. Amma asked, "Son, what is it you want to tell Amma?"

"I would like a violin," he said shyly.

"Son, do you know how to play a violin?"

"No, I haven't learned how to play one. However, I really want to play the violin. I've learned classical music, and if I get a violin, I can learn to play it on my own. I know that if Amma blesses me, I can achieve anything."

The boy's innocent words must have touched Amma's heart. She called me immediately. "Śri-mon, bring your violin here."

I had been given a violin not too many days before. Although I had been playing the flute, I had tried to learn how to play the violin too when I got it. There was another reason behind my newborn interest in playing it. I had once seen Amma playing the violin. A man had put a violin in Amma's hands so that she could bless it. It was then that I heard Amma play a song. When Amma said, "Son, Gaṇapati Swāmi taught Amma how to play the violin," at first I didn't understand what she was saying. I started pondering about the size of the violin that Lord Gaṇapati would have been playing. Divining my thoughts, Amma said, "Hey, idiot! Not Lord Gaṇapati, but Gaṇapati Swāmi!"

After some time, I understood what she meant. Gaṇapati Swāmi was a devotee from Kollam, one among the earliest group of devotees. He had a desire—to somehow teach Amma how to play the violin. He also clearly explained why he had this desire. He felt that he should create an opportunity for devotees to see and hear Devi Herself, who was Goddess of the Arts, play a musical instrument. Gaṇapati Swāmi asked Amma directly, "Child, may I teach you how to play the violin?"

The Lord has no qualms about putting on the jester's robes for the sake of the devotee's happiness! Amma happily agreed to learn the violin.

What ordinary people perceived in Amma was the form and disposition of a young girl. That's why many addressed her as "Little One." For devotees, to see Amma sport like a mischievous child was to experience moments of untold bliss. The next day, Gaṇapati Swāmi came to teach Amma the violin. Gaṇapati Swāmi was aware that while learning how to play the violin, Kunju might insist on being given piggyback rides. Therefore, he knew that he had to be on his guard. Amma's responses always varied according to the beliefs of devotees. If someone called her "Child," she would respond with "Father" or "Mother." If she were called "Mother," Amma would probably call that person "Son" or "Daughter." Those who perceived the nature of both the mother and child in her would address her as "Ammachi-kunju." A few like Gaṇapati Swāmi saw in Amma the Goddess Herself.

He had to admit defeat in the very first class. Amma, who was ready to learn the violin, requested Gaṇapati Swāmi to play a song. He started playing a hymn to Amma, whose face exuded the majesty of Devi. As soon as he started playing, he noticed Amma getting absorbed in samādhi. As he played, gazing in rapture at Devi, tears would spill from his eyes. Every day, Gaṇapati Swāmi would come to teach Amma the violin, and the same thing would happen. He was thus blessed to see Amma in samādhi countless times. Gaṇapati Swāmi must have absorbed the blissful vibrations of samādhi.

"Did you eventually teach Amma the violin?" some asked Gaṇapati Swāmi later.

"I learned," he quipped.

"What did you learn?" they asked again.

"I learned that one cannot teach Devi."

It was a meaningful reply. We are the ones who have to learn from Amma's every move. That is how the Guru teaches us all that we cannot learn. She comes down to our level and enacts Her līlās. It is out of compassion alone that She wears these guises.

When a devotee passed his violin to Amma to get it blessed, she played a song for us to hear. That's when my desire to learn the violin sprouted. Some days later, a man gave me a violin. With Amma's permission, I accepted the gift. I made various attempts to learn the violin. A violin teacher from Karunagapaḷḷy also came to the āśram. I rejoiced, seeing how Amma was orchestrating various situations to enable me to learn the violin.

It was while my violin lessons were thus progressing that Amma said, "Śri-mon, bring your violin here." Amma then handed my violin to that boy. I decided that the flute was more to my tastes and aptitude. Thus, my violin studies came to an end.

Just a few weeks later, when I saw a photograph on the front page of the newspaper, I was stunned. It was the photograph of the first-prize winner in violin playing in that year's State Youth

Festival; all the newspapers featured him prominently. It was none other than the boy to whom Amma had given my violin and her blessings!

"Awaken, Children!"

30

Why did God create this sorrowful world? Why is human life so fraught with grief? Why does God create high walls of obstacles in the path of life?

These questions arise in the hearts of many believers in the world. At critical junctures of life, they inadvertently ask, why has God given us such a sorrowful life?

Amma says, "Children, there is no sorrow in God's world. He is the embodiment of bliss."

Even if we try to show darkness to the sun, it won't be able to see it—there is no darkness in the sun's world. Similarly, there are no sorrows in God's world. He is not responsible for the problems that the darkness of ignorance creates.

So, is there no solution to our distressing experiences? There certainly is, Amma says. There is a solution to all our problems.

From God's standpoint, these sorrows aren't real, even though they seem real to us. This confusion is the basis of all our sorrows. As far as we are concerned, the pain and suffering we are experiencing are real. That's why God needs to come down to the level of human beings as Guru. Yet, divine incarnations can still remain at the level of the divine, though moving among the common man and woman. For this purpose, they hide their glories and assume the guise of ordinary human beings.

Suppose we imagine a wall between God's world and the human world. The door that connects the two worlds is the Guru. In other words, She inhabits both worlds, knowing the secrets of both. The Guru is one who knows both the sorrowful world of the common person and the bliss of divine experience. She is waiting to disclose to us the secret of Liberation from the travails of samsāra, and to remind us of the endless potentialities of human life. She intoxicates the multitudes of devotees with divine love. We may already be praying to God, but we can't be sure that He has heard our prayers. However, Amma has descended into our midst in response to all our prayers, in a form that is easily visible, the very embodiment of love, compassion and self-sacrifice, radiating all the divine attributes, and emitting to millions of people the golden rays of hope.

Although God is always with us, we are unable to perceive Him through our senses. In order to experience Him, we need to transcend the realm of the senses. As far as the ordinary person is concerned, this isn't easy. That's why God has to take a form perceivable by the five senses. Through Her own life, the Incarnation shows us how to be free from the sufferings of life—this is what Amma is doing. Mahātmas, who have attained *pūrṇata* [Fullness], have nothing more to gain. Yet they can be seen working ceaselessly. Amma is also working ceaselessly to set an example to the world, to teach us the value of time, to make us aware of the great tasks that can be accomplished in a brief life, and through these tasks, to train us so that we can reach the fullness of God-realization. All our actions reflect our expectations. Selfishness vitiates these actions. Amma's actions, in contrast, are resplendent with the beauty of selflessness. They exude the sublime majesty of detachment.

Amma listens to our sorrows patiently, and tells us how to be free of them. She also tries to point out the eternal solution to these problems through spiritual counsel. If, in our dreams, we think we are sick, we will go to the dream hospital. The dream doctor will administer some medicine. In this way, the dream sickness will receive a dream healing. If, in our dreams, things are stolen from our house, we will lodge a complaint at the dream police station. Once the dream police have recovered the stolen goods, they will return them, and we will be relieved. In a similar way, thousands of people come to see Amma to get temporary relief from their sorrows. Amma solves their problems. When someone who is ill gets cured, he feels greatly relieved. The job seeker is relieved when she gets a job. Some are relieved when they finally get married. Others feel relieved when their financial situation improves.

Through the power of Amma's sankalpa, our small problems are resolved, but many more problems await us; such is the nature of the world. The solutions we find are all temporary. When we realize this, we will surrender to the Guru and take refuge at Her feet in order to enjoy permanent peace. The Guru shatters all our desires. Things that seem attractive from afar may, when we draw near, seem far from attractive! Once, a man hearing captivating sounds issuing from musical instruments walked in the direction of the music. The sounds were coming from a distance. How beautiful, he thought! When he drew near, he stood listening carefully—it was the sound produced by the beating of many big drums at the same time. Heavy sticks were being used to pound the big drums. And when he went even nearer? The thundering beats were enough to shatter his eardrums! The sound wasn't as sweet as what he had heard when he was far away. His enthusiasm disappeared, and he wanted to run for his life!

Many things in the material world that seem attractive to us today may become distasteful tomorrow. Experience will prove this. There may come a time when we will sigh, recalling all those things for which we wasted our whole life. That's why Amma says, "Children, we must be prepared to learn from the experiences of our lives and correct our mistakes. Instead of remaining on the floor after a fall and crying, we should try to get up."

Amma advises us to soar ecstatically to the heights of spirituality, seeing failure as the harbinger of success. If Amma is there to support us, victory is certain. We must reach the realm of the Self, which is beyond the body, mind and intellect. We must attain Fullness. It's foolish to desire to remain in the cradle forever, like a baby. The father and mother will want the infant to grow up, study and reach the peaks of life. Likewise, God too must be expecting certain things of us.

Mother Nature is waiting for the glorious moment when each one of us will attain Fullness. We can discover the path to everlasting peace if we can become receptive to the Guru's boundless grace.

Amma says that there is but one solution to all sorrows. Awaken! Wake up from this sleep! "Awaken, children!" This is what Amma advises. We needn't fear, seeing the terrors of the dream world; they won't affect the awakened one. However, there needs to be someone nearby who isn't sleeping to awaken the one wailing over the nightmare—that's the role of the Guru. The whole world is sunk in the slumber of delusion. The Guru is attempting to awaken everyone. Yet the world ridicules and persecutes mahātmas who do only good to the world, even today. Unaffected by all this, that Ganges of Love, the very embodiment of self-sacrifice, continues flowing toward all.

Glossary

Abhishekam—*Ceremonial bath, usually given to deities in a temple.*

Ādi Śankarācārya—*Saint who lived about five centuries before Christ, and who is revered as a Guru and chief proponent of the Advaita [Non-dual] philosophy, which holds that creation and Creator are ultimately one.*

Acchan—*Malayāḷam word for 'father.' Its vocative form is 'Acchā.'*

Ambāḍi—*Place where Lord Kṛshṇa grew up.*

Amma(chi)—*Malayāḷam word for 'mother.'*

Annapūrṇeśvari—*Goddess who dispenses food that leaves us sated.*

Antaryāmi—*One who dwells within all beings.*

Arccana—*Chanting of a litany of divine names.*

Āśram—*Monastery. Amma defines it as a compound of two words, 'ā' and 'śramam,' meaning 'that effort' (toward Self-realization).*

Ātma—*Self or Soul.*

Avadhūta—*An enlightened person whose behavior is often eccentric and at odds with social norms.*

Avadhūta Gīta—*Sage Dattātreya's advice to King Yadu, which takes the form of eight chapters of verse.*

Bhagavad Gīta—*Literally, 'Song of the Lord,' it consists of 18 chapters of verses in which Lord Kṛshṇa advises Arjuna. The advice is given on the battlefield of Kurukshetra, just before the righteous Pāṇḍavas fight the unrighteous Kauravas. It is* *a practical guide for facing a crisis in one's personal or social life, and is the essence of Vedic wisdom.*

Bhajan—*Devotional song or hymn in praise of God.*

Bhāva—*Divine mood or attitude.*

Bhakti—*Devotion.*

Brahmā—*Lord of Creation in the Hindu Trinity.*

Brahman—*Ultimate Truth, beyond any attributes; the omniscient, omnipotent, omnipresent substratum of the universe.*

Brahmacāri—*Celibate male disciple who practices spiritual disciplines under a Guru. (Brahmacāriṇi is the female equivalent.)*

Brāhmin—*Member of the priestly caste.*

Circumambulation—*Walking around an object such as a shrine, one of the ritualistic forms of worshipping that object.*

Crore—*One crore is 100 lākhs (1 lākh is 100,000), i.e. 10 million.*

Dakshiṇa—*Honorarium given to the Guru as a token of the disciple's gratitude and appreciation.*

Darśan—*Audience with a holy person or a vision of the Divine.*

Deity—*God or goddess in the Hindu pantheon. Hindus believe that there are a total of 33 crore [330 million] deities. This may be interpreted as meaning that the one indivisible Godhead can take on an infinite number of forms.*

Devi—*Goddess / Divine Mother.*

Devi Bhāva—*'The Divine Mood of Devi,' the state in which Amma reveals her oneness and identity with the Divine Mother.*

Dharma—*Literally, 'that which upholds (creation).' Generally used to refer to the harmony of the universe, a righteous code of conduct, sacred duty or eternal law.*

Durga—*One of the forms of the Goddess.*

Gaṇapati—*see Gaṇesh.*

Gaṇesh(a)—*Another name for Gaṇapati, the elephant-headed God, son of Lord Śiva. Invoked as the remover of obstacles.*

Gopi—*Milk maiden from Vrindāvan. The gopis were known for their ardent devotion to Lord Kṛshṇa. Their devotion exemplifies the most intense love for God.*

Guṇa—*One of three types of qualities viz. sattva, rajas and tamas. Human beings express a combination of these qualities. Satvic qualities are associated with calmness and wisdom, rajas with activity and restlessness, and tamas with dullness or apathy.*

Guru—*Spiritual teacher.*

Gurukula—*Literally, the clan [kula] of the preceptor [Guru]; traditional school where students would stay with the Guru for the entire duration of their studies (a period of about 12 years), during which the Guru would impart scriptural and academic knowledge as well as spiritual values.*

Haṭha Yoga—*Branch of Yoga that deals with physical exercises aimed at harmonizing body, mind and soul.*

Ilanji—*Flowering tree Mimusops Elengi.*

Ishṭa devata—*Preferred form of divinity.*

Jagadambika—*Mother of the Universe.*

Jagadīśvari—*Goddess of the Universe.*

Jaganmāta—*Mother of the Universe.*

Japa—*Repeated chanting of a mantra.*

Jīvātma—*Individual Self or Soul.*

Jñāna—*Knowledge of the Truth.*

Jñāni—*Knower of the Truth.*

Kaḷamezhuttu—*Decorative pictures of deities drawn on the floor with colored powder. Kaḷamezhuttu songs are hymns about these deities.*

Kaḷari—*Generally refers to a temple that does not enshrine an idol. Here, it refers to the ancestral shrine of Amma's family, where Amma used to hold darshans, including the Kṛshṇa Bhāva and Devi Bhāva darshans.*

Karma—*Conscious actions. Also, the chain of effects produced by our actions.*

Kārtika—*Name of the third constellation of stars, the Pleiades.*

Kārtika lamp—*Lamp lit on the day of Kārtika.*

Kauravas—*The 100 children of King Dhritarāshṭra and Queen Gāndhāri, of whom the unrighteous Duryodhana was the eldest. The Kauravas were the enemies of their cousins, the virtuous Pāṇḍavas, with whom they fought in the Mahābhārata War.*

Kāvaḍi—*Decorated arched pole that devotees of Lord Muruga carry during Taipūyam.*

Kṛshṇa *–Principle incarnation of Lord Vishṇu. He was born into a royal family but was raised by foster parents and lived as a young cowherd in Vrindāvan, where He was loved and worshipped by His devoted companions, the gopis and gopas. Krishna later established the city of Dvāraka. He was a friend and advisor to His cousins, the Pāṇḍavas, especially Arjuna, whom He served as charioteer during the Mahābhārata War, and to whom He revealed His teachings as the Bhagavad Gīta.*

Kṛshṇa Bhāva—*'The Divine Mood of Kṛshṇa,' the state in which Amma reveals her oneness and identity with Lord Kṛshṇa.*

Kunju—*'Little One.' Some devotees used to call Amma 'Kunju' or 'Ammachi-kunju.'*

Kuṇḍalini Śakti—*Spiritual power, personified as a snake coiled in the mūlādhāra cakra, a psychic center of spiritual power* *located near the coccyx, at the base of the spine. During the process of spiritual awakening, the snake of spiritual power rises through the spinal column and ultimately reaches the sahasrāra, or crown, cakra, envisaged as a thousand-petaled lotus; this is when one attains spiritual enlightenment.*

Lalita Sahasranāma—*Litany of 1,008 names of Śrī Lalita Devi, a form of the Goddess.*
Lākh—*100,000.*
Līlā(s)—*Divine play.*

Māḍan—*Demon-like demigod.*
Mahā—*an intensifier. For example, a mahājñāni is a great or illustrious knower of Truth.*
Mahābali—*see Oṇam.*
Mahābhārata—*Ancient Indian epic, composed by Sage Vyāsa, depicting the war between the righteous Pāṇḍava clan and the unrighteous Kaurava clan.*
Mahātma—*Literally, 'great soul.' Used to describe those who have attained the supreme spiritual realization.*
Malayāḷam—*Language spoken in the Indian state of Kerala.*
Malayāḷi—*One whose mother-tongue is Malayāḷam.*
Mānasa Pūja—*Worship done mentally.*
Maṭh—*Hindu monastery.*
Māyā—*Cosmic delusion, personified as a temptress.*
Mīnākshi—*Another form of the Goddess. This form is enshrined in a temple in Madurai; hence the soubriquet Madurai Mīnākshi.*
Moksha—*Spiritual liberation.*
Moḷ—*'Daughter' in Malayāḷam.*
Mon—*'Son' in Malayāḷam.*
Mudra—*Gesture formed by the hands and fingers, and having a mystical import.*

Mūlādhāra Cakra—*see Kuṇḍalini Śakti.*

Muṇḍu—*Cloth men tie around the waist, used for covering the lower half of the body.*

Muruga—*Son of Lord Śiva. His divine vehicle is the peacock. Also known as Subrahmanya.*

Nāga—*Serpent. Nāga temples enshrine snake gods. Hindus worship all beings as embodiments of divinity.*

Om—*Primordial sound in the universe; the seed of creation.*

Oṇam—*Kerala's harvest festival. One of the most popular festivals, it is celebrated over 10 days. It is associated with the legend of Mahābali's encounter with Vāmana. Mahābali was a kind and just ruler whose utopian rule endeared him to all his subjects. His only shortcoming was that he was too proud of his generosity. Once, while he was giving away items in charity to his subjects, a young Brahmin boy, Vāmana, approached him and asked for land that could be measured by three paces. Seeing his small size, Mahābali patronizingly agreed. Vāmana, who was actually none other than Lord Vishṇu, grew. With one pace, he covered the entire earth. With the second, he covered all the other regions of the universe. Having nothing else to offer him, Mahābali offered his head for the third step. This gesture symbolizes the surrender of the ego. Lord Vishṇu banished him to the nether world and became the guard to Mahābali's abode. It is said that on Oṇam, Mahābali comes to earth to see how his former subjects are doing.*

Pāda Pūja—*Ceremonial worship of the feet of an honored person, usually a Guru.*

Pañcabhūta—*The five [pañca] elements [bhūtas] that are the material cause of creation. The five elements are ākāś [ether], vāyu [air], agni [fire], jalam [water] and pṛthvi [earth].*

Pañcāmṛtam—*Sweet pudding made from five ingredients.*
Pāṇḍavas—*Five sons of King Pāṇḍu, and the heroes of Mahābhārata.*
Pappaḍam—*Thin, crisp cake made from black-gram flour.*
Paramahamsa—*Exalted saint.*
Paramātma—*Supreme (Cosmic) Self, the oversoul.*
Parameśvara—*Literally, 'Supreme God,' an epithet for Lord Śiva.*
Parāśakti—*Supreme Power, personified as the Goddess or Empress of the Universe.*
Pārvati—*Consort of Lord Śiva.*
Pāyasam—*Sweet pudding.*
Prāṇa Śakti—*Vital force.*
Praṇava—*The mystic syllable 'Om.'*
Prārabdha—*The fruits of actions from previous lives that one is destined to experience in the present life.*
Prasād—*Consecrated offering, usually of food.*
Pūja—*Ceremonial worship.*
Pūrṇam / Pūrṇata—*Full or Whole / Spiritual fullness.*
Pūrvāśram—*Literally 'previous āśram.' Those who have embraced the monastic path cut off ties with the life they led before. They refer to their biological family members or the house they lived in before joining the monastery as being part of their pūrvāśram. Thus, 'pūrvāśram mother' means biological mother (as opposed to spiritual mother).*

Rajas—*see Guṇa.*
Ramaṇa Maharṣhi—*Enlightened spiritual master (1879 – 1950) who lived in Tiruvaṇṇāmalai in Tamil Nāḍu. He recommended Self-inquiry as the path to Liberation, though he approved a variety of paths and spiritual practices.*
Ṛshi—*Self-realized seer or sage who perceived mantras in their meditation.*

Sādhana—*Spiritual practices.*
Sādhak—*Spiritual aspirant or seeker.*
Sahasrāra Cakra—*see Kuṇḍalini Śakti.*
Samādhi—*Literally, 'cessation of all mental vacillation;' oneness with God; a transcendental state in which one loses all sense of individual identity.*
Sankalpa—*Resolve, usually used in association with mahātmas.*
Samsāra—*Cycle of births and deaths.*
Sanātana Dharma—*Literally, 'Eternal Religion,' the original name for Hinduism.*
Sannyāsi—*Monk who has taken formal vows of renunciation (sanyāsa); traditionally wears an ocher-colored robe, representing the burning away of all desires.*
Satguru—*Literally, 'true master.' One who, while still experiencing the bliss of the Self, chooses to come down to the level of ordinary people in order to help them grow spiritually.*
Sattva—*see Guṇa.*
Satya Yuga—*see Yuga.*
Seva—*Selfless service.*
Sevak—*One who engages in seva; volunteer worker.*
Śiva—*Lord of Destruction in the Hindu Trinity.*
Svapna Darśan—*Divine visitation in a dream.*

Taipūyam—*Day of pūyam (pushyam), the eighth lunar asterism, in the month of Tai (mid-January to mid-February). This day is traditionally dedicated to Lord Muruga. Votaries carry a kāvaḍi, adorned with peacock feathers, to propitiate Muruga. Many kāvaḍi bearers dance. Some pierce their bodies with spears or tridents. Some, as part of their vow, walk on a bed of burning coals.*
Tamas—*see Guṇa.*
Tapas—*Spiritual penance or austerities*
Tejas—*Spiritual radiance.*

Tīrtham—*Consecrated water.*
Trikāla jñāni—*Epithet for an enlightened being who knows everything about the past, present and future, i.e. the three time frames.*
Tuḷasi—*Holy or sweet basil (Ocimum Sanctum).*

Upanishad—*Portions of the Vedas dealing with the philosophy of Non-dualism.*
Upavāsa—*Literally, 'to live near' (the Lord); often used figuratively to mean fasting.*

Vaḷḷickāvu—*Place where the Amritapuri āśram is located. Amma is sometimes referred to as 'Vaḷḷickāvu Ammā.'*
Vaikuṇṭha—*Abode of Lord Vishṇu; sometimes used figuratively to mean heaven.*
Vāsana—*Latent tendencies or subtle desires within the mind that manifest as action and habits.*
Vāstu śāstra—*Indian science concerned with the positioning of objects in order to harness the flow of positive energy and divert the flow of negative energy. Similar to Feng Shui.*
Vedas—*Most ancient of all scriptures, the Vedas were not composed by any human author but were 'revealed' in deep meditation to the ancient ṛshis. The mantras composing the Vedas have always existed in nature in the form of subtle vibrations; the ṛshis attained such a deep state of absorption that they were able to perceive these mantras.*
Vīṇa—*Traditional Indian stringed instrument.*
Vishṇu—*Lord of Preservation in the Hindu Trinity.*
Vriścika—*Fourth month in the Malayāḷam calendar.*

Yajña—*Sacrifice, in the sense of offering something in worship.*
Yakshi—*Demigoddess.*
Yama—*Lord of Death.*

Yoga / Yogi—*'Yoga' means union with the supreme being. A yogi is one who has attained that union or is on the path leading to that transcendental oneness.*

Yoga Vaśishṭha—*Compilation of teachings by Sage Vaśishṭha, the Guru of Lord Rāma, who is one of the incarnations of Vishṇu. An ancient text dealing with the philosophy of nonduality through stories.*

Yuga—*Age or epoch. According to Hindu cosmology, the existence of the universe (from origin to dissolution) is characterized by four ages. The first is Satya Yuga, during which dharma or satya [truth] reigns in society. Each age sees the progressive decline of dharma. The second age is known as Treta Yuga, the third age is known as Dvāpara Yuga, and the fourth and present age is known as Kali Yuga.*

www.ingramcontent.com/pod-product-compliance
Lightning Source LLC
LaVergne TN
LVHW051549080426
835510LV00020B/2919

* 9 7 8 1 6 8 0 3 7 0 7 7 5 *